CORONATI(

England Th

C000141451

CORONATION STREETS

England Then and Now

CHRIS ARNOT

This edition published 2023 by:
Takahe Publishing Ltd.
Registered Office:
77 Earlsdon Street, Coventry CV5 6EL

ISBN 978-1-908837-28-8

TAKAHE PUBLISHING LTD. 2023

In memory of my parents, Mavis and Ron Arnot, who gave me everything despite having nothing at the time of the coronation.

Acknowledgements

This book features childhood memories from one end of England to the other. In one chapter we're not far from the Scottish border, in two others somewhere on the south coast. And in between we touch down in Manchester, Birkenhead and Bradford. Staffordshire and Derbyshire as well. Not forgetting Nottingham, Birmingham and Coventry.

The latter has been the most important of those places in terms of research.

Why?

Because, as I may have written before, the most recent City of Culture is really a city of cultures. It's full of people from somewhere else with good stories to tell. Oh yes, and I just happen to live there along with my beloved wife Jackie whose memories of coronation day in Birmingham turned out to be more graphic than mine.

We've lived in other places too, including London and Ludlow. But we spent most of the 1970s in Nottingham where our three daughters were all born. The youngest of them has since moved back there. And it was while visiting her and her husband and children that I caught up with old friends at Trent Bridge cricket ground. One of them, in turn, introduced me to friends of his with evocative memories of childhoods in a post-war world very different from the one we live in seventy years on.

Perhaps it's time to mention those who've shared those memories from places near and far.

They are: Betty and Tony Lewis, Bruce Walker, Anne-Marie Chapman, Barbara Goulden, Professor John Lucas, Maggie Smith, Clive Rowe, Professor Jan Read, John Rubidge, David Kershaw, Philip and Perry Wild, John Jackson, Jean Prescott, Margaret May, Jean Jeffree, Sheila Heathcote, Kate and John Holmes.

Many thanks to all. And, indeed, to my publisher Steve Hodder for his diligent work in putting together yet another book.

Contents

Rain Stopped Play

Two loud noises woke me regularly in those distant days when I was a small boy in south Birmingham. One was the hooter signalling a change of the night-shift at the nearby Austin car factory. The other was a man screaming.

Well, it was the early 1950s and the war with Japan had only finished in August 1945. Our near-neighbour had been a Japanese prisoner-of-war who had witnessed atrocities that those of us lucky enough to have been born after 1945 could never have imagined.

Or so my parents had told me in hushed tones when I asked them to explain all that screaming. It would be many years later before I'd fully understand what they were talking about. All I knew for now was that evidence of war was everywhere.

Men with lost legs hobbled around on crutches, or sometimes one crutch only if they'd lost an arm as well. Bomb sites cratered the surrounding landscape here and there. They'd provide useful hiding places for war games as well as cowboys and "Indians", as Native Americans were called in those days. Like the Germans or "the Japs" in our comics, they were always portrayed as the villains.

Our parents seemed to talk of little else but "The War" when they got together with friends. Ex-servicemen tended to keep quiet about the horrors that they'd been face to face with. But even war-time civilians had seen, heard and felt fears that we "baby-boomers" had been spared.

It was in this context that the nation was preparing for its first great celebration since VJ Night. Queen Elizabeth II had ascended the throne in 1952 when she was twenty five and I was three. Her coronation the following year is among of my earliest memories.

I remember being in the front room of the house next door with the curtains drawn, trying to peer over the heads of other cross-legged children at a small screen showing grey moving images dotted with white spots. The screen was set in a sizeable surround of what I would later discover was walnut veneer.

Our neighbours were one of more than four million families who'd invested in a new-fangled television set to be able to watch the Queen being crowned.

It would be many years later before my parents could afford such a luxury. Although we were considered comparatively posh and my father was an accountant by trade, he spent most of my childhood in bed.

Sometimes the bed was at home where he coughed interminably. And sometimes the bed was in a sanatorium two interminable bus-rides away.

Yes, Dad suffered from tuberculosis, and "TB" was considered incurable at the time. Thankfully, streptomycin would save his life. Eventually. But for now and for some years ahead the only remedy was considered to be fresh air – something of a rarity in Birmingham at a time when the chimneys of factories and foundries were belching smoke day and night.

Needless to say, smoke was hardly confined to the West Midlands. "The only time when the hills around Lancashire towns were clearly visible was during 'wakes week', when the factories shut down and almost the entire population decamped to Blackpool," wrote Nick Tiratsoo in *Blitz to Blair: A New History of Britain*.

Soot from chimneys large and small settled on the window ledges, lace curtains and doorsteps in urban areas all over the country. Most houses were still reliant on open fires. Less so in the summer months, needless to say, and the Queen was finally crowned on June 2, 1953.

But not even the new monarch of an old empire and commonwealth could arrange for the sun to beam down throughout her special day. Apart from trying to see the tiny TV screen in next-door's front room, my other main memory of the coronation is of finding myself sheltering in a neighbour's garage. Our street party had become one of many disrupted by rain.

Thankfully, other baby boomers have more graphic memories of that day. Most are slightly older than me, one or two a few months younger. And you can read about those memories in the chapters to come.

*****

At this point I should, perhaps, confess that I am not a fervent royalist. Not that I had anything against the late Queen. Or indeed her eldest son, who finally inherited the throne aged seventy three. But I can't pretend to feel easy about a system that bequeaths us a head of state by accident of birth.

The British class system may have changed profoundly since the more formal fifties, but it remains weighted towards inherited wealth and privilege. And that will remain the case as long we bow and scrape to whoever was "born to reign over us".

My attitude has long been that nobody has a choice where they're born any more than what colour they're born. It's what you make of your life that counts. And I've met many who've made something of their lives against incredible odds.

Okay, okay, that's enough of the politics. By now you may well be wondering why a far-from-keen royalist would want to write a book about the coronation.

The simple answer is that the older you get the more the past comes back. Twenty years ago I wrote a piece for the Society section of *The Guardian* reflecting on how different this country looked, felt, sounded and smelled fifty years on from the coronation. Another twenty years on and those differences feel even more marked.

To quote from that piece, "The output of the BBC's brassy Light Programme and plum-in-the-mouth Home Service was conveyed through 'wirelesses' the size of large bread bins with surrounds of polished wood. Washing machines were a rarity, but most homes had a heavy, metal mangle which squeezed wet sheets at the risk of crushing fingers in the process."

Our mangle was sited somewhere between the kitchen side door and the coal shed. It was in a glass-roofed storage area that my Mum fondly referred to as the "veranda". She yearned for a washing machine. And a fridge.

Both would be delivered one day. So would a telly. But not until my parents were "back in the office", by which time the 1950s were drawing to a close.

Some of our neighbours in our cul-de-sac of "semis" could afford "washers" and fridges. Many earned "good money" at "the Austin" or Cadbury's. Harold Macmillan's statement to the lower orders that they'd "never had it so good" may have struck a chord with them.

But that much-quoted prime-ministerial line was delivered in 1957 when a new materialism was beginning to manifest itself among the working class and their families. Some, like our neighbours, had managed to get their foot on the housing ladder. Others had moved into new council flats or houses with indoor toilets and baths.

No more boiling endless kettles to fill those tin tubs that used to hang on the back of many a kitchen door.

The coronation had been four years previously when post-war austerity was still all too evident. So if I can't remember what I had to eat on coronation day it's probably because it was decidedly unmemorable. A spam sandwich, perhaps?

I should be so lucky. Or not. To this day I shudder at the memory of spam. Even by the 1960s it was still a regular school "dinner" – battered spam at our school, served with lumpy spuds and soggy overcooked cabbage.

Rationing of meat, including bacon, wasn't finally lifted until the year after the coronation. And bacon was the basis of the "full English breakfast", one of the few British dishes worth celebrating. Roast beef and Yorkshire pudding was another. Mind you, the "Yorkshires" tended to be on the large side, designed as they were to fill up the kids and leave most of the meat for Dad.

The word "cuisine" originated across the Channel where the French have long harboured an array of national dishes. So have many other countries in Europe and Asia.

Seventy years on from the coronation and there are no end of programmes on British television celebrating what has since become our own vibrant and varied food scene. But that's only because we are now a multi-cultural country.

There was much more uniformity about our population in those post-war years. Wearing a uniform, after all, had been part of life for a large percentage of the population during the two world wars that had plagued this planet during the first half of the twentieth century.

Once back in "civvies", most men seemed desperate to blend in. As I wrote in that 2002 piece in *The Guardian*, "The dark suit was *de rigeur* at both ends of the social scale. Savile Row's version may have been hand-cut from the finest material, but a 'gentleman' didn't want to draw attention to himself. Nor did most manual workers, for that matter. On Saturday nights and Sunday lunchtimes, pubs were full of men who had replaced their workaday overalls with white shirts, regimental ties and something bought off the peg from Montague Burton or the Fifty Shilling Taylor."

It took a long time for derisive attitudes towards other men who dressed and looked different from them to change. And in many cases it never did. The teddy-boy craze came in the second half of the fifties. So did increasing numbers of men and women who had the effrontery to have different coloured skin to the home-grown defenders of "this island race".

Never mind that the British Nationality Act of 1948 had declared that all Commonwealth citizens could have British passports. Never mind that the Act was designed to counter the chronic post-war labour shortage.

Fifty years after the Empire Windrush set sail from the Caribbean in '48, I interviewed four of those who had been on board. They had many recollections of racism from employers, fellow employees and boarding-house owners.

Twenty years on and nothing much had changed. In 1968 Harold Wilson's Labour government felt impelled to pass another Race Relations Act to strengthen the one they'd brought in three years earlier.

Birmingham became a major centre for immigration. And Handsworth, a suburb to the north of the city centre, became a magnet for those from the Caribbean and the Indian sub-continent who wanted to live close to people of their own community – hardly surprising in the context of the hostility that they'd faced in pubs and working men's clubs as well as their own workplaces.

But that trend was still in its infancy in the early 1950s when Brewery Street, Handsworth, a long-gone row of terraces just off the main Soho Road, was preparing to celebrate the coronation. My wife Jackie spent her early years there. She's a few months younger than me and her fourth birthday wouldn't come along until a week and two days after the Queen's crowning. Yet her memories of June 2, 1953, are somewhat more detailed than mine, as we're about to discover.

Hands, Knees, Aunt Scrubs a Daisy

A fter the Queen was crowned, so was Jackie Ault – as winner of the Brewery Street fancy dress parade. She was dressed as a daisy. But she had not been a happy little flower earlier in the day. Not while she was standing on the draining board in the kitchen having her knees scrubbed by Auntie Violet, a deeply religious spinster who went about the task with the fervency of one trying to cleanse a simple soul.

"It really hurt," my wife recalled seventy years on as we looked back on that coronation day of pleasure and pain in sunshine and rain.

Jackie's parents had been bombed out of two previous homes in inner-city Birmingham and had been only too grateful to find sanctuary in a humble terraced abode in Handsworth, with welcoming neighbours next door and nearby.

No bathroom, mind you, and the toilet was outside in the yard. A tin bath hung on the back of the kitchen door and was taken down once a week. Filling it was a laborious business, as many another family would testify. Pans and kettles had to be boiled on blue-enamel stoves or black-leaded ranges.

That's how it was, not just in Brewery Street, Handsworth, but in any number of industrial-towns and inner-city terraces all over the country. And it was in that context that children's ears, necks and knees were looked upon as something that could be properly cleansed, like the front doorstep.

I knew this all too well, having not just parents but aunts and uncles painfully probing my "lug-holes" with face flannels. Regular ear-peering was inevitably followed by the dreaded words, "You could grow potatoes in there."

At least Auntie Violet was an assiduous sewer as well as knee-scrubber. "She must have spent ages making my costume," Jackie mused. "I was covered in large petals of white crepe paper with a yellow centre made out of velvet."

The velvet had been supplied by Jack Ault, Jackie's father and Violet's brother, who made luxurious padded boxes to show off diamond rings and pearl necklaces. His workshop was down the road in Birmingham's Jewellery Quarter.

As for her first prize of a doll's tea set, that was presented by her next-door neighbour, otherwise known as Uncle Fred.

Could they by any chance be related?

No. But in those days neighbours and adult friends of the family were often dubbed as "Uncle" or "Auntie" as a token of respect. And there was more than enough respect for Uncle Fred as one who had been captured at Dunkirk and been forced to spend much of the following five years labouring down a Polish coal mine.

On being told that he was "missing, presumed dead", his wife Maude refused to believe it. She carried on raising money to send to prisoners-of-war via the Red Cross. And she was rewarded when her own prisoner-of-war came back to his front door not too long after the end of the war.

Fred went on to get a job as a long-distance lorry driver at a time when thick "smogs" (a combination of smoke and fog) were all too common in winter time in industrial areas all over the country. Once again his family spent long hours fervently hoping that he'd make it home.

He did. What's more, he became a prominent figure in the trade union movement in Brum and a major player in the campaign that resulted in pensioners all over the city being awarded with passes to travel free on the buses.

On coronation day he organised a free bus for children – as long as they lived in Brewery Street. Jackie remembered it as a "charabanc that took us round all the neighbouring streets. Some of them were lined with trestle tables and there were flags and ribbons flying everywhere."

*****

For a little more detail perhaps we should consult with Betty Lewis (née Jeanes), Jackie's long-time friend and former next door neighbour, and daughter of the aforesaid Fred and Maude. After all, she was "nearly seven" rather than "nearly four" on coronation day.

"The coach didn't just go round the streets near us," she maintained. "I remember looking out of the window and seeing that we were just going past Uncle Arthur's house. He was my Mom's* brother and he lived in Smethwick."

It seemed that they'd gone over the border into the distant lands of the Black Country, so named because the cluster of small towns to the north and west of Birmingham harboured foundries as well as factories. As a result, even more soot descended onto the surrounding houses.

After their tour, the children's charabanc pulled up back in Brewery Street where each child was presented with a coronation mug. Plus a coronation crown, if you please – a big silver coin worth five shillings. That would be twenty five pence today. A pittance, you might think.

To a most children in 1953, however, such a sum seemed difficult to imagine. Even half a crown seemed like a "small fortune" to me.

As I write, the government that has bragged that it "got Brexit done" is not yet planning to revert to pre-decimal currency, only pre-decimal measurements. No more metres and centimetres, thank you very much.

Having been carefully measured in feet and inches, Jackie's triumph in the fancy-dress competition took place soon after the coach trip and shortly before children and adults tucked into sandwiches piled high on the trestle tables.

Not even Betty can remember what was in them. She can, though, recall that she was dressed as Britannia "with a long dress and a shield" and that there was a three-tier cake with red, white and blue bunting. "It was probably made by Mrs Billingham who lived two doors from us, on the other side of Jackie's family. Brewery Street was like Coronation Street [appropriately enough]. But there was a school in the middle called St James's that divided 'our end' from 'their end'."

And it was in that school that the adults, no doubt conscious of the afternoon weather forecast, had planned the lunchtime feast and indeed the evening celebrations. Dancing and singing was lubricated by a sherry or two for the ladies and pale or brown ale for the men.

The beer and QC (my future mother-in-law's favourite cream sherry for many years to come) would have been bought from the "outdoor" just up the road. The proprietor, known to one and all as Mrs Wilson, was in hospital giving birth to her fourth child. Another "baby-boomer", as we products of the post-war era would become known.

Typically, Fred raised a toast to Mrs Wilson as well as the Queen. Typically, too, he would have been immensely proud of his son Michael who was studying hard for his GCE O-levels at the time of the Coronation and would eventually make it from a Birmingham grammar school to Nottingham University.

"Dad was a passionate believer in education," Betty reflected. "He'd passed the eleven-plus himself but had no chance of going to grammar school. His father had died when he was ten days old and his mother had nothing. She'd gone into service and farmed him out to people she knew. Some of them treated him cruelly and he finished up in an orphanage in Sutton Coldfield for a while."

Like many another child of pre-war poverty, he was expected to be in manual work by the age of fourteen. And like many another wartime survivor against the odds, he wanted a better life for his own children.

I suspect he was also proud of his daughter who also passed her eleven-plus and went on to make a long-term career for herself in primary education, becoming a deputy head teacher.

*****

Betty now lives in Harborne, one of Birmingham's more prosperous suburbs, in a substantial semi with gardens front and back and the kind of kitchen and bathroom facilities that would have seemed like something out of science-fiction to Brewery Street residents in the early nineteen fifties.

She retired from teaching some years ago. Her husband Tony is retired, too, from a long-term career in the legal profession. The son of a former Welsh miner, he'd gone from another Birmingham grammar school to university in Sheffield before returning to his home city where he became a senior solicitor.

We'll get round to Tony's coronation day memories shortly. But first it's worth reflecting on how many baby-boomers from humble backgrounds made it into middle-class professions within a generation. They had chances that their parents were denied. By war. By economic recession. And, in some cases, by the attitudes of their own parents who liked to think that they knew their place and might issue such decrees as "Don't get above yourselves".

Many of those returning from the Second World War were far more ambitious for their own children to have the chances that they'd never been blessed with. Fred Jeanes (see above) was a classic example.

The brother and sister next door did not pass the all-too-crucial eleven-plus exam, however. They were condemned to secondary-modern schools offering a second-class education. Yet, after much prompting by his parents, Anthony Ault secured a job in a legal firm in the city centre and, many years later, finally became a solicitor.

And Jackie Ault?

My missus now has a masters' degree in applied social science from Warwick University that enabled her to become a social worker. But only after doing A-levels at night school and completing a lengthy degree course with the Open University.

When asked by her academic interviewers why she wanted to do her MA at Warwick, she told them, "Because

I have three kids and I can get here on my bike after I've taken them to school."

$$*****$$

Now back to Tony's coronation day memories from Hodge Hill, a suburb on the east side of Birmingham. The Lewis family lived on Hodge Hill Road where the semi-detached houses would have been described by an estate agent as "compact". Small kitchen and a box bedroom over a small hall. Two more bedrooms, mind you, and a living room and dining room. Plus a bathroom.

"There's posh," as they would have said in south Wales mining villages where, as I mentioned earlier, Tony's father Ken Lewis had grown up in a terraced colliery cottage in Tredegar. We'll be returning there shortly, after the middle one of the three Lewis boys has dredged up his memories of June 2, 1953, when he would have been seven.

His older brother Alec had been born in 1941, shortly before his father had joined the Royal Engineers and been despatched to Singapore. Youngest brother Haydn would have been four or five on coronation day. "He was dressed all in white for the fancy-dress competition with a chef's hat that was quite impressive," Tony recalled.

More impressive than his own headgear, it would seem.

"I was done up as a guard, with red jacket and white belt, but my busby was like a paper bag. A lad called Alan Bothaway, who lived across the road, had a better one."

he added before going on to say, "The event was held in Hodge Hill School, where I was a pupil, and all the local children were all in fancy dress. The rules of the game were that costumes had to be made out of paper or card."

But Tony's big disappointment was not winning the hundred yards later in the day:

"We ran on the outfield at the nearby Ward End Unity Cricket Club where lanes had been marked out. And my Dad was still giving me a briefing about how I should run when somebody blew a whistle. The race was underway and I was about seven yards behind from the start. I did catch up but not quite enough. Gerald Hayes, who lived two doors down from us and was younger than me, was the winner. I was only in second-place."

Still, he was presented with a paint-box to add to his coronation mug. And he also acquired a snake-buckled belt, maybe for winning another race.

It seems likely that such a belt had been bought from Foster Brothers, a popular gents' outfitter at the time. Most boys at primary school had similar belts. They held up grey-flannel short trousers in winter and khaki ones in summer. Both needed holding up as they tended to be bought a couple of sizes too large so that you didn't grow out of them too quickly. And as you grew older, Foster's suitably be-suited shop assistants tended to sidle up and discreetly enquire of you or your father, "Are you all right for socks, sir?"

Memories, memories . . .

Talking of which, did Tony have any memories of seeing the coronation on television?

"We didn't have one. And nobody we knew nearby had one either. But I do remember seeing bits of it at the cinema some time later."

That would have been on the Pathe News – part of the "pictures" package that included the main film, the more second-rate 'B' film and sometimes a cartoon. All for "one and nine" in shillings and pence for adults (under ten "new" pence) and even cheaper for children.

Pathe ran from 1910 to 1990 and during the post-war years it was still presented in the gushingly authoritative tones of Bob Danvers-Walker. During the first half of the 1940s he had kept packed picture houses abreast of what was happening across the channel and far beyond. Newsreel coverage had included the evacuation of Dunkirk in 1940 and the Japanese seizure of Singapore in 1942.

Betty's father had failed to make the former, having been captured by German forces [see above]. And Tony's father had, as his middle son put it, "gone straight out to war, straight to Singapore and straight into Japanese hands as a prisoner-of-war".

*****

Ken Lewis's pre-war upbringing had hardly been idyllic either. The cottage where he grew up in a Welsh valley was not exactly a holiday home. It was one of a terrace close to the colliery from which his father had already been invalided out – the victim of one of the all-too-common accidents at the coal face.

So young Ken became a key wage-earner for the family when he left school and went straight "down the pit" at fourteen.

For the first two years he worked above and below ground with the pit ponies that pulled tubs of coal from the face to the surface. By the age of sixteen he was face-to-face with that face, hewing coal with an axe in hot and dusty conditions that would be considered inhumane the best part of a century later.

Back then it was a way of life. But that life was about to come to an end as the thirties wore on and the pits around Tredegar began to wear out – out of coal, that is. For a young man in his working prime there was no alternative than to get on his bike and seek work elsewhere.

He cycled all the way to Birmingham, the best part of a hundred and ten miles away. Or so Tony told me. Perhaps he'd like to tell us what happened next:

"Dad spent a couple of nights sleeping on New Street Station while looking for work. Then he finally found digs in Hockley over a café that my mother's aunt ran. Yes, Hockley has always been known as 'the Jewellery Quarter' but Mum and Dad had met when he finally found a job at Boxfoldia. And, yes, it was a company that made cardboard boxes."

A lot easier than hewing coal, one imagines. And a hell of a lot easier than being a Japanese prisoner-of-war. "He was on his last legs when the Yanks finally came over the hill and released them. Vitamin deficiency had given him beriberi and he also had malaria. Dad was taken off for convalescence to a hospital in Australia. From six stone he expanded like a balloon.

"Later he went back to being fairly skinny and the severe chest problems continued for the rest of his life as the malaria came back, not helped perhaps by the coal dust that he'd inhaled in his mining days."

Thankfully, he managed to find jobs as park-keeper and postman that required him to be in the open air for the rest of his working life. (Even Birmingham air was fresher than anything that he'd inhaled in a Welsh mine and Japanese prisoner-of-war camp.)

Still, a rare day off to celebrate the Coronation of 1953 must have seemed like a joyous occasion – even if his slightly over-zealous coaching stopped his middle son from winning the hundred yards.

*In Birmingham, England, as in Birmingham, Alabama, Mums are always referred to as Moms.

A 540-mile Round Trip for a View from the Gutter

Hartlepool is a long way from Wembley. Even further from Westminster. A world away, you might well say. Well, nigh-on 270 miles at a very rough estimate.

That didn't stop the Walker family from boarding a train to London on what must have seemed to them a glorious first of June in 1953. Stan and Betty Walker were accompanied by their daughter Jackie and her younger brother Bruce, now a retired academic.

Stan Walker was a Conservative Party agent so, in certain company, he would be known as Stanley. It was a popular name at the time. After all, another Stanley was still making the news on the back pages of some newspapers in the early summer of 1953.

The football world was still abuzz about what would become known as the "Matthews Final". It had taken place on May 2 and the Matthews in question was Stanley of that ilk. Another Stanley, plain old Stan Mortenson, had scored a hat-trick for Blackpool to give them a 4-3 win over Bolton Wanderers – but only, apparently, because of Matthews' dazzling dribbling and pin-point crossing from the wing.

The widely worshipped winger would have been paid the same as his team-mates and the opposition.

Footballers' weekly wages were capped at £14 at that time. A month after the coronation they went up. By a "quid".

Yet fifty seven years later the boots that Matthews had worn in that fabled final were sold at auction by Bonham's for £38,400.

Such a figure would have seemed absurdly astronomical in the year of the coronation. Yet most professional footballers in what is now the Premier League would regard being paid that much for a week's "work" as piffling. The average weekly wage is at least £60,000 today.

Anyway, never mind the Matthews' boots. What about the national crown? And why were the Walkers heading so far south from Hartlepool?

"The main reason why we could go to London," Bruce explained, "was that Auntie Margaret and Uncle Jim lived in Wembley. She was my mum's sister and he was town clerk of what was then a local authority in its own right.

"Both my parents already loved the Queen before she was officially crowned. The coronation was a big thing for them and they'd obviously decided that they should be there."

Apart from anything else, it must have been a blessed relief for Stan Walker to take a brief break. Being an agent for the Conservative Party in a town full of steelworkers, dockers and miners was a fairly thankless task back then.

Nearly seventy years on and the town has a Conservative MP. Or at least it does for now, being part of the "Red Wall" of one-time safe Labour seats that turned blue in the election of 2019.

Back in 1953 the Walkers' train journey went on and on. And on. They were steaming south and young Bruce was in his element. "The journey took about four and a half hours," he recalled. "I remember feeling excited because we were clearly heading somewhere . . . well, exciting."

And that was before he knew what was going to happen the following day, and just how close he would come to the coach carrying the newly crowned Queen.

"I don't remember much about being in Wembley for the first time," he shrugged. "What I do remember is being at the parade that followed the crowning in Westminster Abbey. By then we were in central London, but I couldn't tell you where. All I know is that the streets were thronged with flag-waving crowds. Luckily for me, a kindly policeman noticed me and parted the flag-wavers to wave me through.

"It was like passing through a tunnel of people. The crowds just parted and I sat on the kerb with my feet in the gutter. There were a few other kids sitting there and about twenty yards away was a soldier. He was wearing a red uniform and a big bearskin hat . But it was his feet that eventually drew my attention.

"I remember turning round and saying to the policeman, 'That soldier's shoe laces are undone.'

"He said, 'Oh. Do you think we should go and tell him to do them up?'

"I replied, 'I don't think we can.'

"'We'll leave it then,' the policeman concluded."

The coronation coach duly came past close by and at one point the Queen appeared to be gazing directly at Bruce. Or was it the flag-wavers behind him? Anyway, she waved back an immaculately manicured hand.

The northern boy's other main memory of that memorable day is of being given a toy replica of the coach that he had sat so close to. "There were no royals in it but there was a driver and a footman. I remember taking it back to the house in Wembley and playing with it for a bit. Playing with any toys in those days relied a lot on imagination. Not that you can imagine much with a royal coach. You can't pretend that it's a rocket or a steam engine.

"The coach stayed in our china cabinet for years, along with the coronation mug that all kids were given."

The china cabinet was back home in Hartlepool. For Bruce, going back to the far north was a return to normality. "I wasn't unhappy. Walking past bombsites on the way to school was par for the course. All that colour and sense of being at a 'big thing' had come in the middle of a pretty miserable period for the country. Still, we had a new young Queen and many saw that as a symbol of a new era dawning. If so, it would take a while yet."

Never mind. The family, china cabinet, contents and all, would soon be on the move. First the Walkers went across the north to Carlisle for a few years. Then, when Bruce was thirteen, they moved a long way down south. They were sending themselves to Coventry which was undergoing a massive rebuilding process, harbouring as it did rather more bombsites than most.

For Stan Walker it also harboured potential Tory gains, mainly in what would become its south-westerly constituency.

Bruce would eventually go on to become an economist, researching and lecturing about housing and urban studies at Birmingham University. Although living in London and elsewhere during the early 1970s, he has spent most of his life in the city where his football affiliations lie.

Seeing Coventry City win at Wembley in May, 1987, would evoke memories that eclipsed those of being in Wembley and even Westminster in June, 1953.

A Sing-Song in the 'Bird Aviary' after
Gravy-Flavoured Blancmange

Very few of those featured in previous chapters can remember what was inside the sandwiches consumed at coronation day street parties.

Understandably so.

Food was something to be shovelled down in those days. As the fifties wore on, I can remember shuddering while shovelling down fish paste that had been fished out of a small, gold-rimmed jar and spread on to thinly buttered bread. And that was considered a Saturday treat.

Down in Eastleigh, near Southampton, they had something more sumptuous:

Salmon, if you please. No, not poached or smoked salmon but tinned red salmon. "My grandad worked as a steward on the Queen Mary," Anne-Marie Chapman confided, "so it may have been smuggled off."

No matter. She sighed at the memory of something that must have seemed sublime at the time. "We had it with slices of cucumber. And do you know what: they've been my favourite sandwiches ever since."

Since June 2, 1953, she thinks. But she can't be absolutely sure. After all, she wasn't quite three at the time. She'd been born in September 1950, (on the kitchen floor, as it happened) nine months after her father had finally returned from a distinguished career as a Royal Marine. During the War he'd been everywhere from Burma to the D-Day landings.

And afterwards?

"He ended up peace-keeping in Hong Kong until the shrapnel that had been buried in his leg during one battle or another got worse and he had to come home for an operation in Portsmouth. That was the end of his career in the services. But he managed to get a job at the Ford factory in Southampton, which he hated."

The family name back then was Upton, and former Sergeant Major Upton evidently enjoyed his day off from the shop-floor in order to celebrate the Queen's crowning.

His daughter recalls him playing the piano at a lively evening sing-song somewhere on the grid-shaped council estate known locally as the "Bird Aviary". The Uptons lived on Kingfisher Road and all the other roads had names with avian connections, be it Heron Close or Blackbird Avenue.

Good place for a sing-song, perhaps?

"The men had their suits on and all the adults seemed to be getting happier as the beer and sherry went down and songs like *We'll Meet Again* and *Knees Up Mother Brown* rang out," Anne-Marie recalled.

She also recalled that coronation day had not started happily for her mother. The family cat, it would seem, had

had the audacity to give birth to kittens in a hatbox in the wardrobe that very morning. "Mum got really cross and was in a real flummox. So much so that she picked up the wrong packet and ended up making a blancmange for the street party with gravy granules."

Her daughter may have spilled or spat out the gravy blancmange at some point as she still has a distinct memory of having to change out of her best clothes. "And I'd felt really good in a pale green jumper with a pleated red skirt and matching braces," she told me with a wan smile.

The smile became much wider as a happier memory came to mind.

"I'm fairly sure," she went on, "that I had my first Liquorice Allsort that day. Our next door neighbour gave it to me. Pink coconut on the outside and liquorice in the middle. I can see it now. And taste it," she added before closing her eyes at an evidently ecstatic memory.

(Personally I never acquired a taste for liquorice. Or desiccated coconut for that matter. The only thing I liked about coconuts as I grew older was hurling hard balls at them. In fact, I was eventually banned from the coconut shy at our local church fete for knocking so many out of their containers that I had enough to fill a duffel bag. Then I gave them all away, which at least gained me some much-needed "street-cred" among the "big kids" at "our end" of the cul-de-sac where I grew up.)

Now where were we?

Oh yes, at Eastleigh, near the south coast, where ships near and far were sounding their hooters as if to cheer the crowning of the Queen. They could no doubt have been heard over the sound of BBC Radio, the main source of commentary for residents of the estate where Anne-Marie grew up. "I don't remember anybody on Kingfisher Road having a telly," she said. Nor does she remember she and her friends listening to very much of the radio broadcast that their parents had their ears glued to.

Radios tended to be known as "wirelesses" in those days. They were substantial in size and posh in output. The Light Programme was an exception, offering as it did some lighter programmes for the lower orders through characters such as Wilfred Pickles from Halifax, host of a quiz show *Have a Go*.

Commentary on the Coronation, however, was largely the province of public school old boys and Oxbridge graduates. And they would continue to dominate elite positions on our licence-funded broadcasting corporation for decades to come. Deviations from what was known as "received pronunciation" were rare.

One who did deviate was John Arlott whose Hampshire drawl aged like one of the fine clarets with which he lubricated his vocal chords in many commentary box until his retirement in 1980.

Back in 1953 he was still a year off his fortieth birthday. Somehow I suspect that he would have relished England winning an Ashes victory against Australia for the first time in twenty years somewhat more than being a peripheral part of the BBC's coronation coverage.

Arlott's early life had been very different from that of most "chaps" at the Beeb. He'd grown up in Basingstoke and worked as a policeman for several years. His beat was in Southampton where he'd spent as much as possible of his time "off-shift" watching Hampshire play at their former ground in Northlands Road.

As he went on to become the most distinctive of cricket commentators, he'd talk warmly about the players that he'd chat to on their only day off. No Test or county cricket on Sundays in the 1950s.

So I also suspect that he'd have relished the triumphant England side in 1953 being captained for the first time by a "player", Len Hutton. Players were paid to play cricket. "Gentlemen" were not. They were amateurs with enough money behind them to dally in Test and county games for nothing. And every England captain hitherto had been a "gent". The division between gents and players, marked by a match between them every season, wasn't scrapped until 1962.

That's England for you. Or rather "was". England then and now are very different places. The class system today is far more fluid than it was in 1962 or, indeed, 1953. But it hasn't gone away. And it never will do as long as we have lords and ladies, dukes and duchesses, earls and countesses.

Not to mention queens and kings.

*****

Enough about class. And cricket. That's "Ar lott", as it were. Let's pop back to Eastleigh, near Southampton. As I briefly mentioned earlier, Anne-Marie was born on the kitchen floor of the Upton household. That was in September, 1950, two and three-quarter years before the coronation. Yet in some ways it's a fairly typical tale of the times.

The National Health Service had come into being two years previously, so how did Betty Upton come to give birth at home and on her own?

The answer would seem to be *Gone with the Wind*. It was the film's fault for going on too long – the best part of four hours. And back then audiences were expected to stand at the end of every film for the national anthem. God Save the King came after "the Wind" had finally "Gone".

That seemingly endless epic starred Clark Gable as Brett Butler and Vivien Leigh as the splendidly named Scarlett O'Hara. It had been made in 1939, the start of the war on this side of the Atlantic, and released in 1940.

"Mum had always wanted to see it but, for some reason, she'd never got round to it," Anne-Marie explained. "She was, I think, ten days off my birth date so she and Dad walked down to the Regal to join the queue outside.

"It was a really long film and I think Mum was determined to see the end of it despite the pains in her tummy. These days we'd hop in a taxi but, back then, they had to walk home.

"She got into our tiny kitchen where we had one of those old cabinets with a flap that had to be pulled down to provide a table to work on. She remembered grabbing on to the flap and shouting to my Dad, 'Go and get the doctor.'"

Few phones at home in those days, so the former Royal Marine had to cycle to the nearest red call box, shove in a penny, dial the number and hope to goodness that he'd soon be pressing "button A" to connect.

"By the time he got back, I'd been born," Anne-Marie went on. "Mum literally did it on her own. So I came out, shortly followed by the afterbirth. It landed on my head and she had to pull that off me. Then she got down on the floor with me. All she could see when Dad finally got back was his knees shaking."

After an unconventional birth, life has not been kind to Anne-Marie. Not her later life, anyway. Her husband Mike died of a blood clot caused by an aneurysm when he was sixty one and she was in hospital having part of her foot removed. By then she had finally been diagnosed with diabetes.

She has long since been confined to a wheelchair and has to be taken to hospital for dialysis three times a week. Yet she remains someone of cheerful and chatty demeanour, seemingly relishing opportunities to enjoy the best of a life shrunken by a condition that should have been diagnosed much earlier.

Anne-Marie now lives in Coventry near her son Rob, a computer design technician, and his wife Stacy. A long way from the sea, to be sure. But the squawk of seagulls and the hooting of ships have stayed with her, along with echoes of songs sung round a stand-up piano at a street party some seventy summers ago.

Not forgetting the taste of red-salmon sandwiches and Liquorice Allsorts.

Anne-Marie in '53

Locked Out in the Drizzle from a TV acquired on the HP

Ⅰt wasn't so much a street party as a "back-alley party", according to Barbara Goulden. "There were long trestle tables running between the rear yards of the terraced houses where my auntie lived."

Auntie Mary was one of her mother's several sisters. They all lived in or around Manchester – in Mary's case, on a row of terraces not unlike those on *Coronation Street*. And that seemed appropriate enough in this context as, needless to say, Barbara was describing how those back yards were transformed on coronation day.

Like many another child of post-war and almost post-rationing times, she can't remember what was in the sandwiches strewn along those long trestle tables. What she can remember is that the back-alley party was "a very jolly affair". Once, that is, she'd got over being left out in the rain while the other kids piled into the home of a neighbour who'd acquired a grey- screened TV on "HP".

In those days HP was both a sauce, made near Villa Park in Birmingham, and a source of ready money. The initials stood for hire purchase. And whatever you'd hired to purchase, the money had to be paid back over a certain period of time. With interest.

"My Dad didn't believe in HP," Barbara confided. "He only wanted to buy things he'd saved up for. So I was eleven when we had our first telly."

On coronation day she was six and evidently not fast enough or sharp-elbowed enough to make it through the back gate of the neighbour's house. Gate was soon latched, back door shut. Then it started drizzling – hardly a climatic phenomenon on the west side of the Pennines.

"All the other children had vanished and I didn't know where my auntie had gone," Barbara went on. "She might well have been in her own house listening to events on the wireless and assuming that I was with everyone else.

"I hung around outside, hoping that somebody would notice me. But everybody inside was evidently transfixed by the spectacle. If I'd had the courage to walk into that strange yard and knock on the back door, I've no doubt that they'd have welcomed me in. But I was too shy."

Seventy years on and "shy" is not a word that you'd associate with "Barb", as she's known to her many friends. A sociable soul, she may well have had to knock on a few strangers' doors in her lengthy career as a journalist.

She still uses her maiden-name on website theatre reviews, although she has long been married to another former newspaper feature writer, Peter Walters, who had a somewhat different upbringing. The son of a senior officer in the British army, he went to a public school called Haileybury in Hertfordshire.

Pete and Barb have long since settled in Coventry, having worked on its evening paper in its 1980s hey-day. But as he's too young to remember the Queen's crowning, we need her to take us back to that drizzly day in Manchester.

Appropriately enough, her Mum worked in a raincoat factory. Or "mill", as factories were known in those days on both sides of the Pennines – woollen mills on the east side, cotton on the west.

The mills were alive with the sound of heavy machinery. Not on coronation day, however. Like foundries and factories all over the country, the mills were stilled. Yet to this day, Barbara remains baffled as to the whereabouts of her parents on June 2, 1953. Why had she been dropped off at Auntie Mary's?

Maybe they assumed (rightly) that she'd enjoy the back-alley party. And maybe they assumed (wrongly) that she'd be invited in to the house with the sort of "telly" that they wouldn't have for another five years.

One thing's for sure: she spent many a school holiday at the home of this particular aunt, accompanying her at fairly regular intervals up the back alley and through the back gate of the nearest unofficial "bookie".

Bookmaking wouldn't become legal in the UK for another eight years. But there were more than enough places to place bets on the "gee-gees", as long as you knew where to go.

No, Auntie Mary never told Barbara how much she'd wagered. Yes, they'd go back to listen to the race on the radio – or rather the "wireless" on which "Auntie" had heard the coronation commentary.

Her homely terraced house was in Newton Heath, birthplace of some football club called Manchester United. The Gouldens lived not far away in Clayton, a council estate of comparatively modern housing. With bathrooms, what's more, harbouring inside toilets.

Outside there were gardens. Like a lot of men who'd grown up in terraced housing with nothing but a yard to the rear and a step to the front, John Goulden had relished having a small lawn to mow and soil in which to grow flowers, fruit and veg.

"Dad's tomatoes, strawberries and flowers won cups at the local horticultural society," Barbara recalled. Against fierce competition, one imagines. Gardens, parks and allotments had been turned into much-needed plots of swedes and turnips, cabbages and carrots during the war-time Dig for Victory campaign. Now the renters could grow what they liked – the bigger the better for those among them competing for cups.

Gardening, at home or on the allotment, must have been a restorative pleasure for men who had witnessed terrible brutality in landscapes very different from "England's green and pleasant land".

John Goulden had been in the desert at El Alamein when Field Marshall Bernard Montgomery's forces played a crucial role in the defeat of Generalfieldmarschall Erwin Rommel. "Dad claimed that he once waved at Monty," his younger daughter revealed. "He was an engineer in the Eighth Army, following tanks and mending them."

And after the war?

"He became a joiner with a window-cleaning round on the side."

Earned enough, it would seem, to buy Barb a set of encyclopaedias from one of the numerous salesmen who lugged those tomes from door to door in those distant days decades before information could be "Googled" on-line.

"I read endless Greek myths in one or another of those encyclopaedias," she sighed happily. But, no, she didn't go on to study classics at Oxford or Cambridge. Or any other university for that matter.

An untimely bout of chicken pox meant that she started primary school later than her classmates. "When they were all doing maths, I never got it. Then we had a male maths teacher who hit us," she added with a sad sigh that said it all.

Being hit at school was not uncommon in the post-war years and, indeed, for many years after. Smacks on the bare legs with rulers or plimsolls and clouts round the head with bare hands were par for the course. They could be administered to girls as well as boys, by female teachers as well as male.

To cut a long story short, the Goulden girl failed her eleven-plus. But eventually she became a member of the Manchester Writers' Circle after finally making it into journalism through a somewhat circuitous route.

Needless to say, that was a very long way into the future at the time of the coronation. Barbara's sister Rose was some ten years older and spent that special day waiting on tables at a golf club in Marple where another of their aunts was stewardess.

Marple was in Cheshire and Cheshire was considered "proper posh". Auntie Jane lived in a farmhouse on the edge of the course. "One of the local farmer's sheepdogs once put his paws on my chest and knocked me into the open fire," her niece shuddered before adding, "Fortunately, I was fished out pretty quickly with no real harm done."

As the main source of heating, fires were usually blazing or smouldering in the winter months. The nearest most families got to central heating in those days was pushing the paraffin heater into the centre of a floor covered with thin, cold linoleum – or "lino" as it was generally referred to. Fitted carpets were considered positively luxurious.

It seems likely that lino was the prevailing floor-covering in the terraced street in Newton Heath where Barbara spent coronation day and much of her school holidays.

The route there and back was via a former bomb site that had developed into a piece of much-valued open land. It was known locally as The Dingle or "The Tip". Tipping of household rubbish there was not uncommon and one of her early memories was chasing after an older boy, stumbling into a dip in the ground and cutting a leg wide open on a discarded tin.

"I just lay there, waited until my Dad came and found me then took me on the bus to the hospital. I bawled all the way there and back but, funnily enough, I stopped crying while some twenty stitches were being put in."

She does, though, have happier memories of The Dingle-cum-tip. "There was wildlife everywhere and to me it was like being in the countryside."

Never more so, one imagines, than early on a June day in 1953 when she was clad in her "Sunday best" and looking forward to a "back-alley party". As we know, that was shortly before a new monarch was crowned in London and drizzle began falling on a locked-out little girl in Manchester.

Cucumber Sandwiches
and the Roots of Republicanism

T he crowning of Queen Elizabeth II wasn't the only big news on June 2, 1953. Three days previously Tenzing Norgay had become the first man to reach the summit of Mount Everest. But Tenzing was a mere Sherpa from Nepal. The real "conqueror", hailed by Fleet Street and the BBC on coronation day, was Edmund Hillary – or "Sir" Edmund as he would become soon after he too had scaled 29,032 feet.

Hillary was from New Zealand. "Still, New Zealand was Commonwealth and the leader of the expedition was an Englishman, Colonel John Hunt. So that was alright."

And that was the attitude of large numbers of Englishmen and women at the time, as ironically summarised in the direct quote above from *Next Year Will Be Better*, a memoir of England in the 1950s, by John Lucas. Or "Professor" Lucas, as I should really call him.

Apart from being a poet, novelist and much else, he's Emeritus Professor at the universities of Loughborough and Nottingham Trent. He lectured on English Studies at Nottingham University itself for many years and still lives nearby by in an imposing house, the inside walls of which are seemingly lined with books, books and more books.

Back in 1953 he was sixteen and living with his parents at Ashford in Kent. And it's fair to say that coronation day did not rouse any patriotic emotions – from the adolescent Lucas at least.

The previous Sunday had already sparked an argument with his father who had returned from church and proclaimed over lunch that "God so loves the English that coronation day is sure to dawn bright and fair".

As it transpired, June 2 in Ashford "began wet and got wetter", as John put it. He could have stayed sheltered in the home of a neighbour who invited the family and others to watch events on the BBC. But as he recalled in *Next Year Will Be Better*, "quite early I got away".

He was "both bored and irritated by the tedium of watching". That irritation was, apparently, made worse by the hushed and reverential tone of Richard Dimbleby's commentary. Soon young John was trudging around Ashford's empty, puddled streets.

To quote from the book again, "Everywhere was shut up. Cinemas, pubs, shops all closed. It felt unutterably dreary. This was celebration English style . . . I can only say that I know for me that June 2nd 1953 watered republican roots."

And seventy years on?

"You're joking," he chuckled. "I've hated the monarchy to this day." More chuckles. Those republican sentiments, it would seem, have never waned.

He may have been bored and irritated by the coronation but John has plenty of good memories of 1953. After all, he'd started to play the trumpet and cornet in a jazz band. "I only stopped playing five years ago," he confided before going on to tell me that his band had been reprimanded for sitting down while half-heartedly playing the national anthem. In 1953, and for some time after, standing for *God Save the Queen* was obligatory in dance halls as well as cinemas and theatres.

"There was a nice rebellious spirit in the jazz world," John mused before assuring me that teddy boys and girls were already evident in coronation year. "They had a dance called 'the creep' and it was an unbelievably delightful parody of polite dancing," he recalled.

"The men always had a fag sticking out of the corner of their mouths and the women usually chewed gum as they pushed each other backwards and forwards."

At the end of one gig, as the anthem loomed, he remembered one of the teds coming up, removing the fag from the corner of his mouth and shouting, "Just give us another go at the creep, man."

And so they did.

As the fifties wore on, jiving would take over from creeping and rock 'n' roll would become more and more popular, much to the irritation of the generation who'd been through the war.

No uniforms for the "teds". They wore tight trousers, pointed shoes and long jackets. Longish hair was greased down and swept back. And that was just the boys among them.

For those of my slightly younger generation, teddy boys were both intriguing and slightly frightening. Jukebox music thundered from their steamy-windowed cafes. Fights would kick off at regular intervals, not just in dance halls but sometimes in cinemas where they'd slash seats with their flick-knives.

Some would also try to terrify people of Indian and West Indian heritage. Indeed teds featured prominently in the riots at Notting Hill, West London, as well as the St Ann's district here in Nottingham.

Both conflicts happened five years on from the 1953 when, coronation day apart, the youthful Lucas was enjoying playing not only jazz but cricket.

He'd loved the game ever since being taken to Lord's by his father to see the great Denis Compton in the heady summer of 1947. Two of his many books are about cricket. All too typically, one is called *The Awkward Squad*.

Yes, it's about rebels in the English game. Yes, those rebels were usually so-called "players" who refused to be told what to do by the "gentlemen". And, yes, the class system still bedevils what's still called our national summer game. It's rarely played in state schools and the English Test side is largely filled with those who were privately educated.

Would we have such a class system without the royal family?

I think we might guess Professor Lucas's likely views on that thorny issue.

*****

John and I had arranged to meet at Trent Bridge the previous day to watch a Nottinghamshire county championship game. But somehow we'd failed to liaise. (Contacting an octogenarian who refuses to carry a mobile phone is not easy.) Still, you may not be too surprised to learn that the Radcliffe Road End harboured quite a few spectators old enough to remember the coronation.

I was introduced two of them by an old friend and colleague from my long-ago days on Radio Nottingham. One was Maggie Smith, the other her cousin Clive Rowe. They grew up a few doors from each other in a cul-de-sac in the suburb of Basford.

Maggie is a retired social worker and a republican. She broke the coronation mug she was given at school. Not because of republican sentiments (she was six at the time) but because she and her friends were carrying their mugs while "teetering" along an uneven wall. The railings had been removed during the war, as many railings were, to help provide more metal to make armaments. "It didn't help," said Maggie, "that I was carrying other things and we'd stopped at a shop to buy some Spanish liquorice."

Round "our way" it was called "liquorice root" and it was the only form of liquorice that I chewed in childhood. Not because of the flavour so much as the sensation of eating something that looked as though it had been snapped off the lower branches of a tree.

Anyway, it was hardly the lack of a coronation mug that made coronation day somewhat unmemorable to Maggie. She was bored rigid. "I just remember it being a fairly dull affair. We didn't have to dress up or sing songs. Just sat at these long trestle tables eating sandwiches."

Cucumber sandwiches featured prominently, as her equally bored and slightly older cousin Clive recalled. "There was plenty of vinegar on the cucumber. Some bits of tinned fish and pork luncheon meat featured as well. Then it started raining and the food had to be moved into the [community] hall. For a seven-year-old like me it was hardly the world's most exciting event."

Clive then remembered being even more bored by watching the ceremony earlier on the otherwise much-cherished "telly" in the front room at Maggie's house. "Still, we had to be well behaved as our parents were there. Both our brothers as well."

Maggie's father was a police officer, her mother a housewife who would later take a job at the Player's factory where Clive's dad worked.

The cigarette manufacturers were one of three major companies in Nottingham at a time when smoking had yet to be discovered as a prime cause of health problems in general and lung cancer in particular. To say that sales have declined over the past seventy years is putting it mildly. A ban on smoking indoors in public places, including public houses, would have been unthinkable in 1953. Anyway, what's left of Player's output is now rolled up and sent out of the Far East.

Another major provider of employment in Nottingham was Raleigh. Its products were crammed into many a factory bike shed in the early fifties when cars were far less prevalent than they would soon become.

Raleigh's factory was based in Lenton, not far from inner-city Radford, which was then the home of Player's and the novelist Alan Sillitoe. He was one of the so-called "angry young men", as writers from "northern" industrial towns and cities were dubbed by the London literati.

His most famous novel, *Saturday Night and Sunday Morning*, was first published five years after the coronation. Two years later it was made into a popular black and white film – a "kitchen-sink" drama as the new wave of gritty-grey movies were dubbed at the time. Albert Finney played the roguish hero Arthur Seaton who, when he wasn't downing pints or chasing women, worked in a bike factory.

Far more recently, Sillitoe was quoted as saying that the Raleigh factory was part of the "soul of Nottingham". Maybe that was after it closed down and production moved to the Far East.

Which left just one of what you might call the "big three" employers in Nottingham in 1953 and for some decades after. Boots the Chemist may be American-owned but it still has its manufacturing base in Beeston, on the edge of the city.

And Jesse Boot, who massively expanded on his on his father's first herbalist shop in Nottingham's Goose Gate, eventually became First Baron Trent – appropriately enough as he ended up running the company from a building near the banks of that broad brown river.

It's now a pub called *The Embankment*, but Baron Boot's office has been handsomely restored as a function room with oak panelling, stained glass and much brass.

As it happens, pub stands on the other side of Tent Bridge from the cricket ground. Perhaps it's high time to get back to get back to the Radcliffe Road End to listen to a few more childhood reminiscences from Maggie and Clive.

They certainly struck a chord with me. Like them, I'd grown up in a cul-de-sac in the largely traffic-free fifties. Like them, I remember playing all sorts of street games, including knocking on near-neighbours' doors and running away.

And like them, I recall ball games galore in the street. Football in the winter months, needless to say. But also cricket come the summer when the deep-red base of the nearest lamp-post served as "the wicket".

"My brother was always dragging me into bowling at him," Maggie sighed before Clive interjected to point out to me that "she could play as well as any of the lads".

"I carried on playing until I was a teenager," his cousin went on. "Loved it when we went to Skegness and played on the beach."

Ah yes, "Skeggy", otherwise known as Nottingham-on-Sea. As one brought up on the other side of the Midlands, I didn't get there until the early 1960s. But, like Maggie, I also remember playing cricket on that expansive beach. If you connected with a rubber ball, otherwise known as a Sorbo, you'd be despatched to fetch it back and be running for what seemed like miles to the water's edge. To this day it's a place where, as Philip Larkin wrote about the east coast in general, "sky and water and Lincolnshire meet". Eventually.

Clive would go on to play cricket at grounds somewhat more upmarket than Skegness Beach or a Basford cul-de-sac. After captaining his grammar-school side in Nottingham, he moved into teaching and was later coaching in Devon at "schools that were into serious sport".

Apparently, he "brought on" two or three county players, including Hugh Morris who became a big figure at Glamorgan CCC and played in three Test matches for England in the early nineties.

Before moving back to Nottingham after retirement, Clive had become one of "Her Majesty's" inspectors of schools. It was in that role that he met another inspector covering "outdoor education". His name was George Lowe, a New Zealander by birth, and he just happened to have been official photographer on the 1953 Everest expedition.

"Conked out" at twenty thousand feet, apparently, but was there to take pictures of Hillary and Tensing on their return from the summit. He also had stories that, to Clive, "were far more interesting than the anything about the coronation".

A Day Off from the Pit and a Night in the "Brit"

Sweet rationing ended shortly before the coronation. As a result, a little girl in the Staffordshire town of Rugeley was able to savour a flavour that has lingered in the taste-buds of memory for seven decades. Her name is Janet Read – or Professor Read, as I perhaps should call her. After all, she is now emeritus associate professor at Warwick University and an honorary professor at Cardiff Law School.

Back in June, 1953, she was six years old and the youngest of three sisters. Each was presented not only with the standard coronation mug and crown coin but also a sixpenny block of Cadbury's Dairy Milk. And they weren't the only ones.

"All the children in our neighbourhood had the same," she told me. "And that was a big, big deal. I'm still not sure who organised it. May have been the local Labour Party. I am, though, fairly sure that they organised the street party to celebrate the crowning of the new Queen."

She's also "fairly sure", mind you, that the local streets were strewn with trestle tables topped with sandwiches, cakes and jellies on a day other than June 2. Maybe it was the previous or following weekend. Maybe the organisers had looked at the weather forecast. Or maybe some local

Labour members were reluctant to be seen as being too enthusiastic about the royal family.

Party politics in more ways than one, you might call that. It's also pure speculation on my part.

To move on to more certain matters, the post-war Attlee government had been voted out two years previously. Yet Labour still held power in mining areas such as this one. The MP just up the road in Cannock was Jenny Lee, wife of Aneurin Bevan. He will always be remembered as the miner's-son-turned-politician who'd brought the National Health Service into being five years before the coronation.

And as Minister of Arts in Harold Wilson's first government, Cannock MP Lee would lay the foundations for the Open University. Wilson would later claim the OU as his greatest achievement in power.

That, needless to say, was still a long way in the future in 1953 when a block of Cadbury's Dairy Milk was a "big, big deal". If memory serves, they were sixpence in "old money" in the '50s. That would be two and a half pence in post-decimal currency. Now they're 75p, which would have amounted to 15 shillings. They're also considerably smaller. And I can vouch for that, having worked in Cadbury's warehouse to pay off my student debts. Believe me, a cardboard box full of blocks of those chocs still weighed a ton in 1970.

Still, a factory warehouse in a chocolate factory was a workplace altogether lighter, cleaner and airier than having to crawl to a hot and dusty coal face far underground. And that's what quite a few local men in had to do in Janet's childhood. "There were three pits nearby," she recalled, "at Hednesford, Cannock and also Brereton where my grandfather had worked."

As for her father, he'd worked down the pits in the 1930s and early '40s. During the war he was a bridge builder with the Royal Engineers and eventually he became a plasterer by trade. "But at that time you could be laid off in the building trade throughout the whole of the winter," Janet went on.

Like many another in that era, the winter of 1952-'3 had not been a kind one. Thick smogs, particularly in London, had brought on at least 2,850 deaths and thick snow had brought much of the UK to a standstill at times.

Still, the pits were there to "keep the home fires burning" and, paraffin apart, there was little else in the way of heating.

As Janet was saying, "Dad couldn't stand being unemployed so, once Lea Hall Colliery was sunk later in the '50s, he went back down the pit for the majority of the winter. He was a face-worker for a time. But then you were 'paid by the cut' [the equivalent of piece-work in factories] and he felt bad about not being able to keep up with the younger men. So he moved back to a slightly less well paid job away from the face."

At least there were baths and showers at the pit by that time. Miners didn't have to come home and unhook the tin bath from the back of the kitchen door as part of the lengthy process of getting clean. The tin bath was for the rest of the family. And, yes, the toilet was in a back yard shared with other families – the yard, that is, not the toilet.

No wonder coronation day was seen as "big, big deal" by most miners and their families. It was a rare weekday off in the open air for the men. As for their wives, they could take a break from cleaning and shopping to put on their best dresses and, in some cases, peer at the Queen's dress and crown on a small black and white screen.

A couple of families had televisions on the street where Janet lived. One of them lived over the road and invited their near-neighbours to come and join them. "People took food in with them," she recalled, "and my Mum made a cake in the shape of a crown. With Smarties as jewels, what's more. And, of course, that wouldn't have been possible if sweets hadn't been off-ration."

Did the cake taste as good as it looked?

"My mother was a very good baker, so yes."

For her youngest daughter the cake was a rare break from the tedium of the crowning ceremony and the subsequent parade. "I found it extremely boring," she confessed. "A real waste of telly time to me and my sisters. But I do remember some of the conversations that went on. People were talking about the new Queen in a personalised way, as if they were in the know.

"I can remember a friend of mine's mum saying, 'Do you see how sad she looks? That's because she's thinking of her dad, you know.' Then it seemed that all the women were talking about how the Queen's hair never went out of shape. And somebody said that there was this special stuff that they sprayed on it."

Hairspray, it seems, was something of a rarity among the lower orders.

"None of the rest of us had it back then," Janet confirmed before going to recall the telly-watching women "talking endlessly about the embroidery on the Queen's dress train representing the four nations".

At least the bored children present had some coronation-themed toys to play with while their mothers were glued to that twelve-inch screen. Among them were money boxes in the shape of crowns and miniature models of golden coaches with horses attached.

"In a golden coach there's a heart of gold," as Dickie Valentine sang. And that was a big hit record at the time. It would have been available to buy on a very snappable disc of the day that would have had to be played at seventy eight rpm (revolutions per minute).

On-line pictures of Dickie suggest that he definitely had something to keep his hair in place. Almost certainly it was Brylcreem which, as I also see on-line, was apparently invented in a chemical factory in Birmingham as long ago as 1928.

Anyway, let's fast-forward to June 2, 1953, when the Read sisters had what seemed to them a far more enjoyable evening than watching interminable coverage of the coronation.

"Opposite our house was a big pub called The Britannia," the youngest of the sisters confided. "And the couple who ran it were the other ones in our road with a telly. They had two boys, and my sisters and I and two other friends were invited to join them in the top room while the adults were celebrating in the bar downstairs."

The "young 'uns" upstairs were "playing games while consuming pop and crisps". Not surprisingly, perhaps. There was little else on the television that particular evening than repeats of the coronation.

On normal days in the 1950s, children's programmes such as Andy Pandy or Muffin the Mule would came on at five. And once they'd waved goodbye, there was a lengthy gap in the schedule before BBC TV resumed. Patrick Troughton had already been up and running in the first Robin Hood by 1953. Quatermass didn't start until the month after the coronation, and just as well, perhaps. That "terrifying" science fiction thriller might have put the fear of God into Janet, her sisters and friends.

It seems unlikely that they would have been there to stand for the national anthem by 10.15 when the BBC closed down. But they evidently had a much later night than usual.

Their mother had woken them on the morning of the same day to tell them that Hillary and Tensing had reached the summit of Everest. Maybe that news had seemed more important to her than the forthcoming crowning.

"My parents were a bit different from others in our close mining community," Janet mused. "Mum had been a very bright schoolgirl and won a scholarship to teacher-training college. But her own mother was disabled, which meant that she couldn't go. She had to look after the family and she eventually went into domestic service – with her old head teacher and his wife, who thought very highly of her. So she was under their wing and grew up valuing education.

"As for my Dad, he was brought up in a workhouse. His father had died and his mother was destitute. He was sent from Southampton to Staffordshire as a thirteen-year-old boy. That's when he met Mum and her family."

It was hardly surprising that he, too, wanted a better life for his children.

"So," Janet went on, "we girls had parents who thought that education was a good thing, even though they didn't know much about it. We didn't have a telly ourselves until I was sixteen as they thought it would interfere with our homework. All three of us went to grammar school. That in itself was a huge thing as many girls didn't tend to in our neighbourhood. My parents were given a hard time by some neighbours for letting us go.

The idea was: they'll only get married anyway and those school uniforms cost a lot of money.

"Two of us then went into higher education. That was seen as a clear indication that Mum and Dad were off-the-scale mad.

"My oldest sister, Jean, went in to art college, first to Stafford and then to London. I went to Birmingham, initially to do business studies. Then I realised that it wasn't for me and I moved to Coventry to do social studies at what was then the Lanchester Polytechnic."

It's now Coventry University. The city's other university is, for some obscure reason, called Warwick. And that's where she went to do her masters before becoming a researcher and lecturer in social rather than business studies.

Her father's fellow face-workers from Rugeley would have been astonished. So would their wives.

From D-Day to C-Day on the South Coast

B uilding sites were common sights in the post-war years. After all, the Luftwaffe's blitzkriegs had taken a terrible toll on the UK's housing stock. By 1948, however, some fifty four per cent of those British households that had survived the bombing lacked their own bathroom. No wonder the post-war Labour government was hell-bent on building large numbers of council estates. And they weren't the only ones.

The most council houses built in a single year, 219,000, was achieved in 1953 by a Conservative government led by one Winston Churchill. Or *Sir* Winston Churchill, as he became in April of the same year, just two months before the crowning of the young woman who'd lightly laid a sword on his old shoulder.

The Rubidge family had moved into one of those spanking new council houses not too long before the Queen's coronation. In was sited in Littlehampton, a town that had been very much on the front line a few years previously.

Well, the RAF's Ford Aerodrome was to the rear and to the fore was West Beach, one of many along the south coast from which Allied troops had set sail on D-Day.

It was also the centre of covert operations carried out by the 30 Assault Unit, formed by a certain Commander

Ian Fleming. Yes, *that* Ian Fleming – the one whose work became far from secretive in the years after the war. The first of his James Bond novels, *Casino Royale*, came out in 1953.

By that time John Rubidge was seven. He'd been one of 2.4 million born in 1946, soon after many British soldiers, sailors and airmen had returned home and "jumped into bed", as it was later said of the dawn of the "baby-boomer" generation.

His father, Eric Rubidge, suffered badly from asthma and had spent the war working in various administrative offices. Indeed a particularly bad asthma attack had led to him meeting John's mother, Rosamond, who was driving the ambulance that picked him up. By then he'd been posted to Newport in South Wales.

That's where John was born, although he has no memories of it. Like many baby-boomers, one of his earliest recollections is of playing on nearby building sites. Very nearby on his estate in Littlehampton.

"There was a lot of building work still going on around us," he recalled. "I remember a long trough of lurid green liquid that the builders used to dip long lengths of wood into. So we found offcuts and floated them up and down. God knows what that liquid was.

"What I do know is that there were a lot of children on our estate and we used to go foraging on those sites for nails and bits of wood. Our dads made soapbox carts that we trundled down the slopes. After all, there wasn't much traffic then and our road was a dead-end where more building work was going on."

Good place for a street party, perhaps?

Maybe. But coronation day turned out to be a bit of a damp squib, it would seem, as John reflected nearly seventy years on:

"We started with trestle tables outside and we were supposed to be running around and playing games. But we didn't. Instead we went into different houses up and down the street, probably because of the rainy weather.

"At one point, though, I remember looking up and seeing this cake with the model of a crown on it. Probably made of cardboard, but the jewels all the way round the sides were Rowntree's fruit gums. ('Yum, yum, yum.') And the cushion that the crown was laid on was a cake that seemed huge at the time. I'd never seen deep purple icing before. Mind you, beneath all that icing was just an ordinary sponge cake with a layer of jam in the middle.

"I was dressed up as Robin Hood in green felts of various sorts and my four-year-old brother Tim was a clown in a blue all-in-one suit and a pointy hat. It was light blue with black pom-poms all the way down the front. My Mum used to do a lot of sewing. I remember her making blankets out of what had been army khaki."

She also spent time diligently cutting out pictures of the coronation from newspapers local and national before helping her eldest son to stick them in a scrapbook.

"We spent hours putting it together," he mused many decades on. Not that she was a keen royalist, apparently. "For her it was just something to do."

Like many women, she had been active during the war. Now she was stuck at home for much of the day while "hubby" went to work.

"My dad was quite a royalist," John went on. "All his working life he carried a briefcase with 'ER' on it. He worked for the pension service and then for the civil service in Bath. That's where we moved to when I was about nine or ten. By that time Dad was more than a clerk. He was working in a depot of the Admiralty where they developed the Polaris submarine."

A nuclear submarine, if you please. Joseph Stalin had died three months before the coronation, yet the Cold War had resumed not too long after the Russians had made huge sacrifices in the defeat of Nazi Germany. The United Soviet Socialist Republic was still seen as a threat to the United Kingdom as a close ally of the United States. Hence Polaris.

Now let's get back to life in Littlehampton in the 1950s. And never mind what was in the sandwiches on coronation day. Like many another child of the times, John remembers much more the taste of sweets as treats:

"Although our parents never went to church, me and my brother were sent to Sunday school and given money for the collection. But we'd stop on the way and spend most of it on liquorice from the sweet shop."

An even tastier treat was to come when Grandad ("Dad's dad") arrived on Fridays with bars of Fry's Chocolate Cream. Made in Bristol, it was Britain's oldest chocolate bar, dating back to 1866. British pilots in World War Two had been given one each before taking off on bombing raids.

Grandad Rubidge's biggest treat for the family, however, was not chocolate but beef – bearing in mind that meat rationing didn't end until the year after the coronation. Rubidge senior just happened to be an inspector for a meat company called Armour, based in Portsmouth. "And they imported loads of beef from Argentina," John confided. "So we always had great slabs of it on Sunday lunchtimes and cold beef in one form or another all week long."

It was similar at *Chateau d'Arnot* in Birmingham as the fifties wore on and rationing wore out. We'd have beef, or sometimes lamb, on Sundays. Also on Mondays, cold with scallops (sliced and battered spuds). It was cold meat with warm gravy and mashed potatoes on Tuesdays. And on Wednesdays the remains would be minced up for a cottage pie.

Can't remember much about Thursdays but, if you were lucky, you'd get fish and chips on Fridays. All dinners were served around 6.45, the time when *The Archers* went out on the Home Service. Conversation was limited. We were expected to listen to Dan and Doris at Brookfield, Tom Forrest in the gamekeeper's hut, Peggy and Jack at the Bull, Walter Gabriel and Ned Larkin on the other side of the bar.

Time, perhaps, to move on – or at least move back from 1950s Ambridge to 1950s Littlehampton. Over to you again, John:

"One of my clearest memories of being there then was walking through the town with my Mum who stopped to chat with a friend who had a baby. I looked into the pram and I was shocked. The baby was black – or of mixed race, anyway. It was the first time that I'd seen a black child."

A legacy of the war, perhaps, when black American soldiers were among those training on the south coast for the D-Day invasion? Or perhaps not, as most had headed for home soon after VE-Day and any "baby" conceived before then would have been at least three by the time that young Rubidge clapped eyes on him.

Admittedly the Empire Windrush had docked in London in 1948, bringing the first wave of West Indian immigrants. But few, if any, would have headed south. Most would either have stayed in London or moved north to big cities such as Birmingham to take on the factory jobs that they'd been invited to fill by a British government short of labour.

Still, there are always a few exceptions, albeit very rare exceptions in John's younger days. "The only time that I saw black people after we'd moved to Bath was at the jazz club where I used to go."

That changed when he sent himself to Coventry. Or, to be more accurate, in 1966 he became a trainee teacher at what was then the Coventry College of Education. He finished up as head of science at what is now a high-achieving senior school in the inner-city. Many of the school's pupils move on into higher education and, eventually, into comparatively well-paid jobs. And the majority are of Asian descent.

No, racism among employers hasn't disappeared. But the UK now is a very different place from the UK of seventy years ago when the late Queen was crowned and immigrants were arriving from the "colonies" to fill menial jobs in long-gone factories.

Just look at what is now "His" Majesty's Government. As I write, we have our first prime minister of Asian heritage and a front bench in which there are several non-white faces. And that's a *Conservative* government.

Then there's the BBC.

Mastermind is masterfully presented by Clive Myrie whose parents came from Jamaica to Bolton. His father was a factory worker. Clive has also presented the BBC television news on numerous occasions, as have other non-white newscasters. On Radio 4, meanwhile, the news and programme links are often read in the resonant tones of Neil Nunes who was born and brought up in Jamaica.

For all its financial problems, our national public broadcaster is infinitely better than in the days when its presenters were exclusively Oxbridge graduates who seemed to be talking to you down their noses.

As for our national dish, it could be argued that chicken tikka masala is as much a contender as the roast beef that John Rubidge no longer savours.

From Grey TV Screen to Meeting the Queen in Full Colour

The mills had fallen silent for a whole day. And it wasn't even a Sunday. Yet there were no obvious signs of the mill workers spinning themselves into wild celebrations. No street-parties "oop there", a thousand feet above sea level on the council estate at Bradford's Horton Bank Top. Not as far as ten-year-old David Kershaw was aware. Nor was he aware of anybody nearby having one of those new-fangled televisions on which to watch the Queen being crowned.

Undeterred, he boarded a bus into town and a trolley bus out again. It was a journey of not much more than eight miles that took the best part of an hour. Admittedly, trolley buses wouldn't last much longer. In Bradford and many another city they were being phased out in the fifties, along with trams. But even diesel-powered buses struggled to surmount the steep gradients in West Yorkshire's second largest city.

All the same, David was determined to get across town to "Uncle" Billy's house. A comparatively posh house, it would seem. With a TV, what's more. That was the attraction as far as young Kershaw was concerned. He'd never peered at one of those small and fuzzy black and white screens before.

These days ten would be considered by some parents a bit young for a child to travel alone from one side of a city to the other on public transport. Back then, however, there was far less traffic and the risks would have been considered negligible by parents who had survived battles and blitzes

A teacher at David's primary school had "made a big thing of the coronation to come". He'd believed her when she'd told him and his fellow pupils "to see it if you can".

And see it he did, thanks to Uncle Billy who wasn't really an uncle at all. Like "Auntie", it was simply a title that children were expected to bestow on friends of their parents back then. David's dad, Jarratt Kershaw, had grown up next door to Billy and both had gone on to work for Bradford City Council – Billy as a draughtsman and his former neighbour as a rates collector.

So why hadn't Kershaw senior, who'd returned to municipal routine after six years war service in the "Royal" Navy, not gone to watch the Westminster Abbey proceedings with his son?

"My father was not over-impressed by royalty," that son explained. "He wasn't an out and out republican, but he didn't show any interest in it. And his complacency seemed to be echoed by most of the men on our estate. They weren't aggressively against all the fuss around the coronation, just not particularly interested."

Not surprisingly, Alice Kershaw talked a lot more than her husband about the new Queen on coronation day.

"But Mum seemed surprised that a woman was going to become the head of state," David said, shaking his head. "To her it should have been a man. She wasn't exactly a feminist."

Few women were. The coronation was held two decades before feminism began to surface as a serious movement. Yes, women had worked hard outside the home during the war – in factories, on farms, in offices and elsewhere. But once their husbands had returned from the armed forces, they were expected to get back in the kitchen.

David thinks it likely that on coronation day his mother would have had a brief break from cooking and cleaning to sit in the hallowed sanctuary of the front parlour and listen to events unfold in faraway Westminster. But "dinner" would still be expected to be on the table by lunchtime, even if her beloved son was on the other side of town, apparently entranced by his first encounter with a television.

"It was also my first introduction to that sort of music – the singing in Westminster Abbey and the procession that followed. I didn't understand it, but enjoyed it enough to stay through the whole procedure."

It seems likely that there would have been a brief break for dinner – or even "lunch, as it may have been called in that posher part of Bradford. It would almost certainly have been cooked by the "cleaner", who later became Uncle Billy's wife. Billy had been a bachelor for nigh-on sixty years but his elderly mother, who lived at the house, had decreed: "You've got to get married as I'm not going to live for much longer."

Young Kershaw knew that he couldn't stay for much longer as the afternoon wore on and the trolley bus awaited. He had to be home for "tea". It would almost certainly be a salad, the tomatoes sliced in half with a sprinkling of sugar, despite post-war rationing of castor not coming to an end for a few months yet.

Meat was still rationed as well, but Alice Kershaw had her ways of acquiring slightly more brisket than most. Buttered up the butcher, it would seem.

On Sundays it was served hot, albeit with small portions for David and his younger sister Ann. They were expected to fill up on enormous Yorkshire puddings with a lake of gravy inside the steep banks of its raised sides.

As for the brisket, that was expected to last for most of the week, served cold on Mondays, Tuesdays (coronation day or not), Wednesdays and Thursdays. With mashed potatoes, mind you, soggy cabbage, lumpy swede and some Yorkshire chutney. As for the dessert, that was almost invariably rice pudding.

No wonder the family looked forward to Fridays. That was when Alice came up with the *spécialité de la maison*, as they rarely said in Bradford. Before getting married, she'd worked in one of the city's chip shops where she'd learnt to fry a piece of haddock or cod in proper fatty batter and wrap it up in the back or front page of the Telegraph and Argus with a "penn'orth" or two of chips.

Nobody could cook fish and chips like Mrs K. Certainly not the landlady of the boarding house in Mablethorpe where the family decamped every year. It was the Bradford holiday fortnight when the mills fell silent, not just for a day but for two whole weeks from the beginning of August.

Two months had passed since the coronation. Yet on two Saturdays running the main street of this Lincolnshire coastal town was alive with the sound of ongoing celebrations. David remembers leaving his parents on their deckchairs and his sister in the sand before crossing the road from the beach to join in events on the main street.

"There was loads of music with brass bands to the fore and clowns acting as cheer-leaders," he recalled. "And on one of those Saturdays, six or seven mounted police came along. They made a big fuss about the Queen's enjoyment of horses and then dismounted to let us kids enjoy stroking the horses." He paused before adding, "That was really my biggest celebration of the coronation."

Mind you, he was among a host of children encircling Bradford Park Avenue cricket ground that was "heaving with people" when Queen came a calling the following spring. "I'd had to join a choir and, for some reason, we had to sing Nymphs and Shepherds while she stood up in a Land Rover that was being driven round the edge of the ground."

Little did he know at the time that one day he would meet the Queen personally and be presented with a CBE for services to education. After all, he'd recently failed his eleven-plus and was struggling at a secondary-modern school run by a sadistic head teacher – no doubt screwed up by wartime experiences, like many another. He seemed to revel in thrashing children within an inch of their lives.

David left school with no qualifications whatsoever, expecting to make his living as a professional footballer. After all, he was on the books at Huddersfield Town and playing alongside some young shaver called Denis Law in the under-18 side.

Until, that is, a new manager called Bill Shankly took over and told him that he wasn't going to make it as a pro'. That was before going on to tell him that he really should be a teacher. He even paid for him to acquire the necessary qualifications. Eventually. And eventually he became not just a teacher but the head teacher of the most successful school in Coventry.

Retirement didn't stop him. He went on to work for the Department for Education, helping many a failing school in cities such as Leicester and, yes, Bradford. Hence the CBE.

So what was it like meeting the woman whose coronation had been something of a damp squib on the estate where he'd grown up?

"We were shepherded into Buckingham Palace where they split us up. The OBEs were regarded as the plebs, a bit lower down the order. Only about twenty of us were about to become CBEs and we went into a separate room with the knighthoods. One of them was about to become Sir Ian Botham.

"Barry Humphries was there as well and when they started playing the national anthem he proclaimed rather loudly, 'I think we should have Waltzing Matilda as well.'

"One of the retired guardsmen organising the day turned round and growled, 'Mr Humphries, are you taking this seriously or not?' Still, he didn't calm down much until the knights and dames had been through and it was the turn of we CBEs.

"I was astounded how small the Queen was, even though she was standing on a box. But she had a word with everybody. What she said to me was, 'How do you cope with those naughty children'? I just said, 'You have to be firm and occasionally give them a bit of tough love.'"

To which the reply was "Thank you very much."

- David Kershaw's autobiography *Thanks Shanks, how Bill Shankly bought me an education and Denis Law kicked me in the shins*, was published by Takahe in 2017. That was ten years after he became David Kershaw CBE and sixty four years after he'd travelled by trolley bus to watch the crowning of the Queen on the tiniest of screens.

Stan Matthews and the Fabled Final of Fifty Three

Those few, those "happy few" who could afford to buy a television set some time before the coronation may or may not have switched on to watch the fabled FA Cup Final of '53. Probably not in the case of those from the upper-middle classes who had been privately educated and brought up to play rugby.

To them the "other sort of football" was for the "hoi-polloi". The post-war Labour government may have done much to help reduce inequality yet the British class system was still alive and sticking its nose up.

For the vast majority of the population, however, the match between Bolton Wanderers and Blackpool remained quite a talking point long after it was staged – on May 2, 1953, as it happened. And as mentioned in Chapter Three, the new Queen, exactly a month away from her crowning, was sitting patiently in the royal box waiting to present the cup.

Her sporting preferences were for horse-racing and show-jumping. But even she may have become somewhat engaged by the drama unfolding on the field below.

Bolton were comfortably leading 3-1 with just over twenty minutes to go. Then one Stanley Matthews started to weave his wing-side magic. Footballs were heavily leathered in those days, filled with air from bicycle pumps and stitched up with rutted lace that could be very painful to head. One of many myths around Matthews was that he could cross a ball with the lace turned away from whoever's forehead thrust forward to stick it in the net.

Another Stanley, Stan Mortenson, scored a hat-trick in the final that finished with Blackpool as 4-3 winners. Yet the game would be referred to henceforth as "the Matthews final".

He was "the Ronaldo of his day, albeit on twenty quid* a week", as Philip Wild recalled. Those wing-side weavings and pinpoint crosses were very much in his mind a month later. Yes, it was June 2, 1953. And like many another local lad and lass from Sandiacre, a small town in south-east Derbyshire, he was desperately trying to relieve his boredom.

"Half of Sandiacre's children seemed to be there," he said as he remembered being crammed cross-legged on the floorboards of his auntie's house. The curtains were drawn. The recently rented television was on. And the ladies on the settee behind were jabbering away about the procession leaving Westminster Abbey. They could just about see what the Queen was wearing as they peered at a nine-inch screen peeping from "a massive wooden cabinet".

It seems that the auntie who'd acquired the TV on the HP, otherwise known as hire purchase, was Philip's father's sister. "Mind you, I don't remember Dad or any other men watching the ceremony."

Nor does he remember any street parties round and about. Maybe that was a consequence of wet weather. Earlier that morning, ten-year-old Master Wild had cycled through the rain from his parents' house some ten minutes ride away.

"In those days families tended to live quite close to each other," he mused. "You'd get married and live two streets from your mum and dad. Our house was on a narrow country lane that's now the approach road to junction twenty five of the M1," he went on to explain.

He cycled back there well before the BBC's coverage of the coronation had come to an end. "If we'd have been watching football, I'd have stayed," he confided.

Philip, who now lives in a village ten miles from Sandiacre, remains a Derby County season ticket holder to this day. Saw his first match at the Baseball Ground in October, 1952, apparently, when the glories of the Brian Clough era were still twenty years away. "I went with my dad just as he'd gone with my grandad and I used to take my two sons," he told me.

These days he goes with his wife Perry. We'll be hearing about her coronation day memories shortly, but first tell us a bit about your father, Philip:

"He wasn't much of a drinker so there were no great celebrations after the coronation. Mind you, he'd have to have been up early the next morning to cycle to work at Spondon, just outside Derby. Every working day for over fifty years he cycled eight miles there and eight miles back."

Even during the war?

"He tried to sign up for the navy and was asked what he did for a living. On being told that he made artificial silk, they sent him straight home. The recruiting officer told him that he had to carry on doing his job as we desperately needed parachutes. So my dad was in the navy for all of two days."

Frank Wild's wife and Philip's mother, Phyllis, just happened to be the daughter of Fred Tate and the sister of Maurice Tate. Both played cricket for Sussex and England. Only one Test in the case of Fred who died in 1943, the year after Philip was born.

Maurice, however, was a star for Sussex and England, a useful batsman and a very effective fast-medium bowler with a hundred and fifty five Test wickets. Wisden Cricketer of the Year, no less, in 1924. "And he once gave me a signed ball," his Derbyshire-supporting nephew disclosed.

Apart from that gripping FA Cup Final, 1953 was also a memorable year for English cricket. A month after her crowning, the Queen was shaking hands with "twenty two of her subjects, English and Australian, in front of the Lord's pavilion", as Wisden put it.

That Test was drawn. So were three others. But England won the final game at the Oval to clinch the Ashes for the first time in two decades. Under the captaincy of Yorkshire's Len Hutton, the batting would have been predominantly dour and gritty by today's standards.

Nonetheless, those English lovers of the game watching on BBC would have been glad that they hadn't sent back their rented "tellies" immediately after the coronation.

Now let's get back to Maurice Tate's sister and, indeed, Philip's mother, Phyllis. Yes, she was a housewife in his early years. And, yes, she'd done her "patriotic duty" by working "somewhere in (nearby) Long Eaton during the war". The early part of the war anyway. In 1942 she discovered that she was pregnant again for the first time in fourteen years.

"I think my sister was married by then," the product of that pregnancy mused, "and I felt like an only child as my brother seemed so much older. In fact, he just missed being called up for the war. Instead he was did national service soon after that war finally came to an end. Went to Germany and found himself guarding Rudolf Hess (Hitler's deputy) at Spandau Prison."

Back home in Sandiacre, his much younger brother was also in a uniform. Of sorts. "Every boy back then dressed pretty well the same – jumper, shirt and short trousers," Philip reminded me. "I was still in short trousers until I was thirteen."

By that time, three years on from the coronation, he was regularly catching a bus to secondary school. "Three or four double-deckers and many more bikes used to pass by on their way to the nearby Stanton iron works," he said before going on to recall the days when Stanton and Staveley was a major local employer turning out everything from manhole covers to the hooter on the Queen Mary. "Thousands of people worked there and you knew straight away that the ovens had been opened because the sky turned red."

The other major employer locally was the lace trade and that's where Philip worked for fourteen years before going to college in nearby Ilkeston and acquiring enough O and A levels to get into Nottingham University.

He became a social worker eventually. So did Perry. Eventually. They'd married in 1966, an even more significant year for English football. The Queen was back at Wembley once more to present the World Cup to England captain Bobby Moore.

By then it was thirteen years since the "Matthews final". Oh yes, and the coronation. Time, perhaps, for Perry's memories of that day. She was seven at the time and her sister Jill was four. Their father, Oliver Watt, was a wages clerk and a former Grenadier Guard who had been badly injured at the Battle of Monte Cassino in 1944.

"He did get a war pension," Perry remembered, "but every time he went into Nottingham for his annual medical assessment, they knocked a bit off his payment."

His wife, May, worked in a solicitor's office part-time. "And that was frowned upon by some of our neighbours as she had children," her elder daughter went on. "But she was always at the house for us when we came home from school."

Both parents were there for them on coronation day. It seems that all went over the nearby Nottinghamshire border into the adjoining town of Stapleford.

"My grandparents lived there," she explained, "and my grandfather was a dentist. He'd bought (not rented) a television especially for the occasion. They were of a generation that cared for their elderly relatives so his father was there along with two maiden aunts."

There were a lot of "maidens" about thanks to a shortage of men following the first world war. Plenty of widows as well, needless to say.

"Aunt Hannah and Aunt Alice were tall and thin and always wore black dresses with lacy collars," Perry went on to say. "As for our great grandfather, he seemed to think that the Queen was waving at him personally."

Well, he was "into his eighties at the time", which meant that he'd been born during the reign of the last female monarch, one Queen Victoria. It seems likely that this was his first encounter with a television. And he may well have dozed off by the time that the BBC's extensive coverage of the coronation and the carriage parade that followed finally came to an end.

"We must have had some food at some time," Perry reflected, "but I don't remember what it was. No party stuff, that was for sure. We always had a sit-down meal at our grandparents."

One thing Perry does remember about those distant days of the early fifties was her grandfather buying one of the first cars in their road. "The local garage provided the car and the owner stood on the running board, held on for grim death and told him how to change gear while they drove round the block."

Needless to say, the new Queen had no need to take driving lessons. She had her own chauffeur. After all, part of her job was to go on a seemingly endless round of UK and commonwealth tours in the years that followed her coronation, regularly waving to adoring crowds.

There are still plenty of adoring royalists today, needless to say. But, as Philip put in, "The attitude in those days was that the royal family were these absolutely perfect people and everybody should touch their forelocks to them. I remember somebody saying to me, 'You have to protect the royal family. They're better than us.' "

So what's his attitude to that family seventy years on from the coronation and eighty years since he was born?

"I think there's far too many of them and they have far too much money. And the behaviour of some of them has been a disgrace. I'm not saying that I'm a republican but if you trimmed the royals down to about three people, I'd be happy with that."

Perry would seem to agree. "When we were younger everyone accepted the royal family. But then we didn't know enough about it. If it wasn't for the press in more recent times, we wouldn't know what some of them have got up to."

Praise for the press, indeed. Whatever next?

Having disappeared for a few minutes, Perry returned carrying the coronation mug given to her at school nigh-on seventy years previously. In remarkably good condition, what's more.

"That's probably because I've never used it," she smiled.

As mentioned in Chapter Three, £14 a week rather than "twenty quid" was the standard wage for all professional footballers in June, 1953.

Perry's coronation mug - one of few survivors

Another Crowning, Albeit in Birkenhead

B irkenhead, a "ferry 'cross the Mersey" from Liverpool and 230 miles from Westminster, staged its own crowning on June 2, 1953. Not with a gold crown, needless to say. Nor was it inset, like the royal crown, with two thousand eight hundred diamonds, two hundred and sixty nine pearls, seventeen sapphires, eleven emeralds and four rubies.

Like many another, it was a cardboard crown. And it was carried on a cushion by John Jackson, who was five "and three-quarters" and concentrating hard on keeping his feet steady on a triangular-shaped piece of wasteland. Allowing the crown to slip onto the ground may have led to some sniggers and giggles among the watching neighbours. Maybe some irritation, too, from the little girl ahead and the two other girls behind her, holding on to the train of her dress.

John was feeling somewhat constrained around the neck as he was wearing a tie for the first time in his life. "Not sure who knotted it," he said. "All I remember is that I was wearing my best clothes when we came out of the house on the other side of the triangle from our house. We walked down one side of the triangle, turned left and went another fifty yards to a little stage that someone had put up.

"There was a chair, or 'throne', on the stage, for our 'queen' to sit down on and an old lady just behind it. She probably wasn't that old, come to think of it now that I'm seventy four, but she seemed old to me at the time. Anyway, she came over to me, took the crown off the cushion and plonked it on the girl's head. And that was about it."

Well, it was as far as the local coronation was concerned. There was still a street party to come to celebrate the national coronation. But before we get to that, let's find out a bit about the street in question.

"We were close to the docks and they'd been bombed extensively during the war," John explained. "Roads about a mile away had been blown up but, surprisingly perhaps, the old terraced, dockland streets like ours were still intact."

Still the rent man came round once a week. Still the properties were, as John put it, "in very poor condition". Still there was no hot water. Still the tin bath had to be unhooked from the back of the kitchen door on Friday evenings for the family to take it in turns to bathe in increasingly murky boiled-up water.

"The toilet was at the bottom of the yard," John went on. "And in order to get there you had to weave your way through all these hens."

Hens? In Birkenhead?

Not a great surprise, come to think of it. Our next door neighbours had them in Birmingham. So did many other residents of urban areas all over the country. It was a way of getting a Sunday dinner at a time when the end of meat rationing was still a year away and poultry farming on an industrial scale was yet to come.

Chickens for the Jackson family were acquired by John's grandmother, otherwise known to him and his younger brother David as "Nan".

"I don't know where she got them from," John shrugged. "But I remember that she used to come in with a cardboard box full of fluffy little chicks around Easter time. She'd feed them up and, just before Christmas, she'd kill them. Wrung their necks. And it wasn't always an instant kill. One or two would sometimes run around our tiny little back kitchen with their heads at a funny angle. It was no problem for her to finish them off. Then I think she sold off most of them."

Local butchers would have been grateful. So was John's mother, Lilian. Better known as "Lil", she didn't mind plucking and cooking them but tended to flee the kitchen when her mother-in-law began her slaughtering regime.

"Mum didn't like live hens at all," her older son went on, before assuring me that he had no such problems. "I used to go into the hen coop through a little door to collect the eggs. I also hid in there when I was in trouble."

He doesn't remember his mother cooking a chicken for the coronation party. But he's fairly sure that one or two of her cakes would have featured prominently on the trestle tables that ran along the street. After all, she'd been a professional caterer before the war.

Her husband and John's father, Richard Jackson, had finally come home from the war in 1946 – back to the house that his parents had rented since 1910. His own father had died in 1941 but not from anything "war-related".

Private Jackson's war had been lengthy and varied. He'd somehow survived being at battles in North Africa and Italy in time to be back at the southern end of the UK to take part in the D-Day landings.

"He'd had an awful time in the war and common sense says that he would have been screwed up by all that," John mused. "But it never materialised. He was not a violent man in any way at all."

Eventually his father was taken on as an electrician by Birkenhead "Corporation", as the larger local authorities were known in those days. But for a while after the war, he'd pushed a barrow round town as an odd-job man.

John remembers barrows being more common than cars in the early fifties when he felt free to ride his tricycle around surrounding streets with no fear of being run over.

He also remembers that, like many another, his dad had tried and failed to get a job helping to unload visiting ships. "The docks were very important in Birkenhead at the time. A good number of people on our street worked there. But there was a casual labour system. If you knew the selecting manager, you got in. If you didn't, you were just shoved away."

It seems likely that any ships arriving on June 2, 1953, would have remained unloaded and the gates to the docks locked. Dockers and would-be dockers had a day off from the tensions of queueing at those gates.

It also seems likely that few of them had "tellies" on which they or, more likely their wives, could watch proceedings in Westminster. "One of my mother's friends on the next road had a TV," John recalled. But he couldn't recall seeing it himself at all.

Mind you, he may well have seen an abridged version on the Pathe News at one of no fewer than four cinemas within a quarter of a mile of where he lived. Mind you, it seems unlikely that he could have heard much of the coronation commentary had he wished to.

"We used to go to children's films at one called the Ritz on Saturday mornings," he said. "It was absolute madness."

Few children would sit down, it would seem. Few would shut up and listen. And very few could resist shouting derision and "hurling all sorts of things" at the organist who rose from the bowels of the building to serenade the unappreciative audience. "The poor guy would have to play for ten minutes before he went back down again," John reflected with a shake of the head.

What did they throw at him?

"Well, you could buy choc-ices and ice-lollies by then, so it was mainly wrappers and sometimes small sticks."

And "by then", I suspect, the baby-boomers were beginning to enjoy occasional treats that their parents' generation could hardly have dreamt of in childhood.

No wonder coronation day had seemed an unprecedented time of celebration that they made the most of, everywhere from Birkenhead to Birmingham and beyond. Certainly it carried on for some time at the Jackson family home near the docks.

"I can remember being given a hydrogen-filled balloon," John confided. Almost immediately I let go of it and it floated away. I was really upset about that. When I went into the house, somebody gave me another one and told me in no uncertain terms not to let go of it.

"The house was full of people that evening," he went on. "My auntie was a very gifted pianist and there was some singing around the piano. And that was in the 'best room' that was normally never used. It was one of three rooms downstairs, so it may have been a matter of cost – one less fire to light."

He's telling me this while sitting in the back room of a substantial property that he shares with his wife Gill in

West Bridgford, a prosperous borough just south of the River Trent and close to Nottingham Forest's City Ground and Trent Bridge cricket ground.

He's a long-time lover of both games, having first played them with friends and neighbours on the largely traffic-free streets of Birkenhead.

Unlike most of those friends and neighbours, he'd passed the eleven-plus, gone to a nearby grammar school and finished up as an inspector with the Inland Revenue. That was after the three promotions that had led to his move from the north-west to the East Midlands in the mid-seventies, twenty years on from the family's move from the dockland terraces to a nearby council estate. "There were just the four of us," John explained. "Nan stayed behind. I can remember her distress when we moved out."

Still, she had hens and neighbours for company in a house where she'd lived since the end of the Edwardian era. She'd moved in as Edward VII was on his way out and the late Queen's grandfather, George V, was planning his own coronation some 230 miles away in a different world from Birkenhead.

John Jackson as he was in March, 1949, just over four years before the coronation. Note the hen in the pen.

Watching Events on a Twelve-Inch "Big Screen"

The late Queen was looking down on us from a framed birthday card to Margaret. Not Princess Margaret, needless to say, but Margaret May – to congratulate her on her hundredth birthday.

She was now a hundred and one. Mrs May, that is. The Queen had expired at a mere ninety six in September, 2022. And I'd been introduced to the remarkable Margaret almost at the end of that year, shortly before the dawn of 2023 when Charles III would finally be crowned.

Margaret's memories of the coronation of seventy years previously were not coming readily to the surface. She was far better at recalling the street parties that heralded VE Day and VJ Day. Not surprisingly, perhaps, as she had lost her mother and her home in a world war that had gone on for six years.

In the early stages of the war, her family were living in Longford on the northern edge of Coventry. The centre of that ancient city had been largely destroyed in the blitz of November, 1940. Not seemingly content with that, the Luftwaffe had returned the following April for another four nights of bombing.

"We had eight bombs landing straight down our street," Margaret recalled. "They killed no end of people, including my Mum. She'd kept going to the front door to see if the neighbours had come back from work. I kept shouting at her, 'You can't do anything about it, Mum. Why don't you stay here'?"

"Here" was under the kitchen table where she sheltered with her boyfriend. "My Dad had been injured at work, so he lay on his bed and he was alright."

Except that he'd lost his wife. Not to mention his house. The family ended up sharing a two-bedroomed semi-detached in nearby Collycroft, just over the north Warwickshire border and next door to the former mining town of Bedworth where Margaret's niece Jean Prescott has lived for many years.

Jean is a spring chicken of eighty seven and by the time of the coronation that "semi" must have seemed positively spacious. By then it was just her, younger sister Pat and their parents. Auntie Margaret, Uncle Ernie and their baby had moved out. Not forgetting Margaret's sister, another Jean, and her brother Fred.

"There were so many of us at one time that we all had to wash with shaving soap towards the end of each month as the other kind of soap was on ration," Jean Prescott remembered.

She was seventeen by the time of the coronation. But she still harbours fond memories of the Collycroft cul-de-sac just before and just after the war when kids were free to play outside. "Boys and girls used to mix in and we played everything from rounders to hopscotch."

Free from much in the way of traffic, it seems that they were hopping, skipping and jumping. "Scrumping" too. "There was a private orchard behind our house and we used to jump over the fence and help ourselves to an apple each on the way to school," Jean went on.

Like many another in those days, she'd left school at fifteen and found work at Alfred Herbert's in inner-city Coventry. It was one of the world's largest manufacturers of machine tools and her father, Walter Carter, was one of many working in the factory. Jean soon learnt to type and began a lengthy career as a secretary.

"When I started they'd just stopped doing short-hand," she told me. "Bosses would dictate on to a tape recorder. You fed the tape into this machine, put your earphones on and typed whatever was said."

No taping or typing on coronation day, of course. Instead of cycling the best part of six miles to the Red Lane branch of Herbert's, Jean went as far as next door. And stayed there. All day.

The neighbours had not only acquired a television but what you might call a "magnifying screen". Clipped it on the front and – hey presto – it evolved from nine inches to twelve.

Whatever next?

Well, seventy years on and some people that I know have screens not too far off cinema-size. In colour what's more. As I may have said before, having something like that in your living room would have been considered science fiction in 1953.

Watching the Queen being crowned on a "twelve-inch" was undoubtedly a novelty for Jean's generation, even if the curtains had to remain pulled tightly together all day. "Those of us who were young enough had to sit on the floor," she went on to say.

Didn't you get bored?

"Oh no. It was a novelty. Next door, my Mum was making sandwiches. Can't remember what was in them. Things were still hard to get, even though rationing was beginning to come to an end."

Sweet rationing had ended in April, 1949, followed by what you might call a big sugar rush with extremely long queues outside sweet shops. Result: rationing of everything from Smarties to Mars Bars back on again until February of coronation year.

And on coronation day in Collycroft, Jean remembered her Mum also coming up with a jelly and jacket potatoes. "It was nice to have something warm," she added.

Spuds were comparatively easy to come by back then. Even if you were growing your own, you no longer had to Dig for Victory. Having them cooked in their own jackets was something to savour – particularly, as I recall, on November the fifth in the fifties. To this day I can still remember biting in to blackened skins retrieved from the dying embers of bonfires that had lit up back gardens all over the neighbourhood.

Never mind bonfire nights. Let's get back to coronation day in Collycroft. Beyond the closed curtains, apparently, flags fluttered all around the cul-de-sac. But the main celebrations seemed to be inside the living room of the house with the magnified TV.

To quote Jean, "everybody was discussing what the Queen was wearing and how lovely she looked". At least the women were. There were few men present. "A lot of them would have been in the pub," she assumed before going on to tell me that "Mum was very much a royalist". Despite being of Spanish descent, it would seem.

Her oldest daughter doesn't have a clue how Berenguela Letiti had met Walter Carter. "You didn't ask questions in those days. And we were expected to keep quiet at meal times."

But she does know that her mother was called "Lettie" during the war when she'd worked in one of many local factories turning out munitions. And after munitions were no longer required, she'd moved to a company called Kennings, making "Masonic wear".

Aprons and ribbons among them, apparently. Yet the Freemasons, to give them their full name, were for gents only. Admittedly they staged occasional "ladies' nights" of dinners and dances, but regular meetings of Masons involved secretive rituals that dated back centuries.

There were also secretive handshakes that confirmed membership when "gentlemen" were introduced to one another. A hitherto stranger would know that he could do business with the bloke that he'd just shaken hands with. The Queen's husband Prince Philip was one, Winston Churchill another.

Not too many miners became masons, I suspect. And as Jean reflected at some point in our conversation, "there were miners in our road and every road round here". She then went on to tell me tell me that her uncle Ernie (Margaret Day's husband) had been an "overman" at nearby Newdigate Colliery, having taken a step back from the coal face with a back injury.

Mind you, coal faces in Warwickshire were higher than most. Rich in coal, too. In the months before and after the coronation, they would have been turning out many a ton as rationing was coming to an end. Environmental concerns were a long way in the future, despite the thick fogs and outright "smogs" spreading above ground.

Incidentally, the Newdigate who gave his name to the pit of that name was one of a wealthy family that built mills as well as sank mines. They were based at Arbury Hall, just off what is now the A444 between Nuneaton and Bedworth.

One Mary Anne Evans, the daughter of the estate's land agent, was born there in 1819. She would become better known as George Eliot, author of *Middlemarch* and

Mill on the Floss, thought to be based on Arbury Mill where she played as a child.

Her family home on the Arbury estate is now a Beefeater Steakhouse.

Jean's family home has been in Bedworth for over fifty years. She "crossed the border" from Collycroft two years after the coronation when she married Alf Prescott, another employee of Alfred Herbert's.

They'd met in a car crammed with other employees of that machine tools manufacturer on their way to a match at Highfield Road, home of Coventry City FC from 1899 until 2005. Might even have been an evening kick-off as floodlights were first installed there four months after the coronation.

At some point she must have had to confess to Alf and other Coventry supporters that her first love, on the football front at least, was Leicester City. "My Dad first took me to Filbert Street when I was twelve," she explained. "You could get a bus from Collycroft that went straight through to Leicester. Mum and Pat used to go shopping and we'd meet up after the game in Lewis's (department store) for a so-called 'Football Special Tea'."

Not very special, it would seem. "Don't ask me what was in the sandwiches," she said, echoing many a memory of British food in the fifties – rarely memorable, even after rationing finally came to an end.

Mind you, I can remember to this day what you might call football teas at our house as that decade wore on and coronation day became a distant memory. My Dad had finally recovered from TB and was back earning money. On Saturdays at five pm precisely he would be bent over his pools coupon as the theme music from *Sports Report* issued from the Light Programme while I was faced with the task of seeing off a fish paste sandwich.

Only by forcing that sandwich down could I be rewarded with a rare treat – a Kunzle cake, its thick chocolate shell filled with some form of butter cream. A great way to take away the taste of fish paste, for sure. Just as I was sure that, at some point before the football results reader John Webster reached the Scottish second division, Dad would screw up his pools coupon and toss it into the fire.

Many years later, Jean would spend Saturday afternoons with her headphones on while typing up football reports from Highfield Road and elsewhere. Everything had to be done at top speed in order to hit the streets as soon as possible with "The Pink", the sports paper of what was then the Coventry *Evening* Telegraph.

On weekdays she had to rather more leisurely task of being secretary on the *Telegraph*'s features desk. Sat next to me, as it happened. Well, I was features editor of that esteemed organ when she joined us in 1983, a mere thirty years after the coronation.

The birthday card to Margaret May from the Queen

Fainting on The Mall

Jean Jeffree's close-up photo of the Queen on coronation day went missing when she moved house some years ago. "I was really upset when I found that it had gone," she reflected. "That picture had always given the impression that Her Majesty was waving out of her carriage at me personally."

Yes, it was in black and white. Colour was still a decade away. And, yes, it was taken with a Kodak Brownie. Or so she thinks. Well, it was seventy years ago when Jean Davis, as she was then, boarded a Euston-bound train at Coventry Station on what must have seemed to her and her mother, Hilary, a particularly glorious first of June.

Both were royalists after all. Both had taken an extra day off work. And both knew it would be a close call to find a place on the thronged pavements on The Mall, close to Buckingham Palace.

It was difficult enough to find two seats in one of the crammed "second-class" compartments on the steam train that chugged into Coventry from Birmingham New Street. The railways had been nationalised five years previously and this one was run by the London Midland Scottish (LMS) branch of British Rail.

Both stations would be rebuilt in the 1960s, as indeed would Euston. But for now they dated back to the early and mid-19th century. New Street had the largest single-span arched roof in the world when it was opened in 1854 – on June the first, as it happened, along with the nearby Queen's Hotel. Coventry's station had opened in the 1830s, making it the first city to connect with London by train.

Alfred Lord Tennyson had made a fleeting visit in 1840 to write a characteristically lengthy tribute to Lady Godiva. His introduction explained how, while waiting for the London-bound return train, he "hung with grooms and porters on the bridge to watch the three tall spires".

Somehow those three spires, if not the cathedral attached to one of them, survived the devastating blitz that came exactly a century later. Of that more later.

For now let's just say that the station would have looked much the same when the excited mother and daughter pulled out in 1953 as when, "coming up England by a different line" the following year, another poet looked out of the window. In *I Remember, I Remember* Philip Larkin exclaimed, "Why Coventry! I was born here".

So was Jean, albeit thirteen years after Larkin and eighteen years before the coronation. She was a "Coventry kid", as she told me when we met in her apartment in the sought-after suburb of Earlsdon. Now eighty seven, she looks back on her teenage life with warmth and fondness for family and friends.

Those friends included colleagues in the Government office where she worked, on the historic highway known as Far Gosford Street. "Before we set off to the coronation," she recalled, "two people from my office said, 'ooh, if you're going to London would you get this for me from such and such a shop?' I said 'oh yes; that's no trouble.'

"But when we got to Euston, we were agog. There was a mass of people and they all seemed to be heading to the Mall. There was no way we could go shopping."

Instead Jean and her mum had to keep their feet and go with the flow, like football fans on the way to the old rib-crushing terraces at the home end. Except that there would have been far more women bound for the coronation street on to which the new Queen would emerge some time on the following day.

Not too many seats on the southbound tube train, needless to say. Jean and Hilary held on for grim death. Back at street level, they found themselves swept along with the crowd once more.

This is pure speculation on my part, but en route to The Mall Hilary Davis may well have glanced up from the surge every now and then to wonder what was going on in the kitchens of those posh hotels that had survived attacks on London by the Luftwaffe. "My mother was marvellous woman and, like my dad, she was a worker," Jean assured me. The coronation trip, it seems, was a rare two days off from doing breakfasts at a hotel in Coventry.

It must have seemed well worth the train and tube fares when they finally found two spaces on the pavement close to the Palace. All they had to do was wait and wait. And wait.

The *Evening News* as well as the *Evening Standard* was circulating all over London in those days and sellers were coming round shouting "Everest conquered; Coronation cancelled".

Oh, that Cockney sense of humour, eh?

"The nice part was that we'd settled down next to a family of Londoners," Jean beamed. "They were so lovely to us There were two men and a lady. We hadn't brought any night clothes but they said, 'Use one of our blankets'. Then we got chatting and one of them told us, 'One thing you must come back to London for is the Trooping of the Colour'."

To her evident regret, Jean never has. Instead she had to watch the "Colour" in black and white for many years. "Mind you, I love sitting here now watching it in colour," she added, gesturing towards a TV screen almost as big as those found in some cinemas back in the fifties.

And back at the coronation?

As she went on to say, "Most people were lying down as the night wore on, trying to get some sleep. And then the police came round telling us that everybody had to get up. It was about three in the morning. As I looked across to the other side of The Mall I saw this lady fainting. So what did I do?

"I fainted too. And, no, I wasn't putting it on. I'd fainted once or twice before. Anyway, the St John's Ambulance crew came, helped me up and took me to St James's Park, not far away. 'Just rest here,' one of them said and they helped me on to a bed. Then I must have fallen asleep while the nearby crowds were still standing up."

Come daylight, it seems, she was still "spark out".

Jean went on, "In the end someone from the ambulance crew was shaking me and saying, 'Come on; you've got to get back to your place'. They knew exactly where Mum was and took me round to get in position again.

"Mum was relieved and pleased to see me back but evidently knew that I'd been in good hands. The St John's crew were nearby. In fact, one of them said, 'Come and stand in front of me'. I was fine and enjoying everything that was going on."

Mother and daughter had long since seen off the sandwiches that they'd brought from Coventry. But there were "passing traders" selling snacks. Jean can't remember what they were. (Thankfully not jellied eels, the *pièce de résistance* savoured in homes and cafes a few miles east of Westminster.)

She can remember the weather being "nice", for a while at least, and having a good view of the royal coach going past on its way to Westminster Abbey. "And, yes, we waited for the Queen to come back. It took a long time but everyone was jolly, singing songs and enjoying the day."

Then it was back to the packed train bound for Coventry and Birmingham, as the following day would be very different. Work beckoned. After a late night would come an early start, particularly for Jean's mother. Hilary Davis would have had to be back in the hotel kitchen – although the "full English breakfast" that guests are offered today, along with other options, might have seemed somewhat niggardly by comparison. As mentioned elsewhere, rationing of bacon didn't fully come to an end until the following year.

And the year after that, 1955, saw the opening of the Leofric where Hilary would move to and work. It was the first hotel to be built in a British city with British finance since World War Two. The cost was eight hundred thousand pounds, a huge sum at the time.

The hotel was considered decidedly upmarket. Seventy five of the hundred and eight bedrooms were en-suite. With connections for electric shavers, if you please. American tourists called in in some numbers. So did the Warwickshire gin-and-Jag set, such was the reputation of the cocktail barman Ray Rastall.

Stars stayed over after playing at what was then the nearby Hippodrome Theatre. Among them were Beryl Reed and Gracie Fields, Harry Seacombe and Tommy Cooper. The latter seemed particularly keen on the cocktails.

The Leofric stood on Broadgate, the square at the crest of Britain's first pedestrian precinct. All these developments were Government-backed and considered symbolic, showing that a destroyed British city could rise from the rubble. The nearby "new" cathedral was even more dramatic symbol, but that wouldn't be consecrated until 1962.

*****

Time perhaps get back to 1953, a year that Jean remembered fondly – not just for having been at the coronation but for the general feeling that life was getting better. Well, she was eighteen and evidently full of life.

"I was very happy at work," she told me. "You didn't have to work too hard in the civil service in those days. We had a drama group and all sorts of other social gatherings. Mum used to say, 'I don't know why you don't take your bed down there. You're always doing something.'

"We used to go dancing at the Matrix Ballroom. There were some big bands there."

Big in size, as dance bands trended to be when waltzing and quickstepping were still in vogue. It would be early in the following decade when up and coming bands – or "groups" as they were known by then – played very different music at the Matrix. One was called the Rolling Stones, another The Beatles.

"After dances in my day," Jean went on, "if nobody took you home, you could walk back. No need to worry about anything."

Well, I suppose that if you and two brothers had spent your childhood in wartime evacuation and seen your home city ablaze in the blitz from a farm in south Warwickshire, other threats of night-time attack must have seemed negligible.

Both her parents survived the intense bombing. Like many another, they had an air-raid shelter in the garden. Her father, Sidney Davis, was an air-raid warden by then, having also survived fighting in the First World War.

It was soon after that carnage on the western front that Coventry's vastly spacious War Memorial Park was laid out. And it was there that Jean started yet another club for colleagues. "I hired one of the courts at the park and started a tennis club. Everyone who joined paid a pound."

That included someone called Doug Jeffree who'd recently moved from Cornwall to Coventry. He was a fireman at the time, like the husband of Jean's friend Edna. "I don't play tennis," he'd protested when it was suggested that he should join. To which his colleague pointed out, "Ah, but the secretary's worth a pound."

You may not be surprised to learn that that's how Jean met her future husband. He'd "courted" her, you might say.

She was widowed some years ago. Pictures of Doug, their two sons Paul and Stephen and four grandchildren could well be among the many framed photos on the walls of her apartment.

But one much-treasured picture is missing. Yes, the long-lost shot of the Queen taken close up on coronation day, 1953.

Pub-Brewed beer in a Jug and a Sing-Song in the Snug

T wo members of what was once the Melbourne family, Sheila Heathcote and Kate Holmes, were back in the Exeter Arms in Derby, a pub in which they'd first spent an afternoon and evening some seventy summers previously. Sheila was twelve at the time and Kate six.

No, they shouldn't have been there. Strict licensing laws prevailed at the time. Pubs were expected to close for around three hours every afternoon and even longer on Sundays. But, hey, this was coronation day and the street party at the block of 1930s council flats across the road had been disrupted by rain.

The licensee Winnie Jackson – "a big, grey-haired woman," as one of the sisters recalled – was evidently a kindly soul. She wasn't going to lock out the women and children from a predominantly male domain on such a celebratory day.

The weather had been dry and sometimes sunny in the morning. Yet many of the neighbours in what was once Exeter Street had chosen to sit indoors. They'd piled into the Melbourne family's terraced house five doors away from the pub.

"We were the only ones in the street with a TV set," Kate confirmed. "Dad bought one specially." Then Sheila confirmed that "our front room was absolutely crammed". Mainly with women and children, it would seem. "There weren't that many men in there," she added, before adding again that "Mum was in the kitchen making endless cups of tea".

Like the licensee of the Exeter Arms, she was a Winifred known as Winnie and, like many another mother, she'd spent the war working in a munitions factory before returning to housewifely work when the "man of the house" came home.

Lance-corporal John William Melbourne came home despite having been injured as a tank driver at the Battle of Monte-Casino. He was soon back in something like a uniform, however, albeit in a navy rather than a khaki jacket. It had brass buttons and "the eagle of Barclay's bank imprinted on each one".

I think it was Kate who remembered that, although it may have been Sheila. Not always easy to tell when two sisters sound similar on the voice recorder. Anyway, Kate, or maybe Sheila, went on to tell me that "Dad was like a bank messenger. This sounds ridiculous now but he used to go from bank to bank with money in a leather bag strapped to his wrist. If one bank needed more cash, he transferred it."

At this point the other sister remembered that he also sported a bowler hat. He must have looked quite distinctive setting off to work. Flat caps and trilbies were far more common in in Exeter Street. Most men would have worked in industrial settings, including a nearby jam factory.

Like many a wife and mother at the time, Winnie Melbourne maintained that her husband had come back from the battlefield as "a different man".

He could still play the piano, mind you. "Dad played it for us every night in the front room," Sheila recalled. Only, mind you, after the distinctive signature tune of The Archers had faded away on the BBC Light Programme, to be followed by the pips and the news read in a voice very different from Walter Gabriel's. That was at 7pm in those days.

The two sisters were expected to be in their pyjamas by then. So was their eight-year-old brother, John. Then they were all expected to march off up the stairs to bed in due order while the former lance-corporal serenaded them with *I Do Like to be Beside the Seaside*.

That may well have been one of the many tunes plonked out by the pub pianist at the Exeter Arms on coronation day afternoon. And evening. "I don't know what time we finally went to bed," Sheila reflected before turning to Kate and adding, "I think you fell asleep in the pub."

Neither can remember whether the pub parrot joined in with the singing. They can, however, remember the parrot's favourite phrase: "He's got the ace of spades."

The old bird seemed to have learnt it from the card-players in the snug, each with their distinctive china beer mugs. Crown Derby, needless to say.

Both sisters first saw the parrot in summer days when they poked their heads through the open top of the stable door harbouring the "offie", otherwise known as the off-licence. They were either with friends, taking a brief break from playing in the street, or with their Mum. Like many another mother and dutiful wife, she'd be lugging a jug to be filled with bitter or mild. Both were brewed on the premises in those days by one Dick Platt.

Dick it was who was called in by the Melbournes to see off the fearsome cockerel that used to strut around their back yard and put the fear of God into the girls when they needed to get to the outside toilet.

"The kitchen was away from the house as well," Kate confided. "In there was a stone boiler that gave us hot water on wash day. And we seemed a bit posh compared with the rest of the street because Dad had a bath put in there."

Sheila then took up the story by adding that "there was a cooker in there as well but Mum also had a range in the house and she cooked mainly on that". And "that", presumably, was where she made endless cups of tea for the neighbours peering and squinting at the nine-inch TV screen in the front room as the Queen set off in her golden coach, turned grey by the BBC cameramen.

The sisters' attitude differed when it came to watching events unfolding in far-away London. Sheila, it seems, was quite absorbed. "It had been drummed into us at school what an important event it was going to be," she said.

Kate admitted that she was bored rigid after a while. "Quite a few of us sneaked out to play," she confessed. Swinging on a rope tied to a lamppost was considered far more fun than sitting cross-legged in the front room watching the slow progress of a horse-drawn coach through streets full of waving crowds in a different world. So was playing marbles in the gutter.

"They were really ball-bearings that we used to steal from the garage down the road," she confessed before going on to tell me that there were pictures of the Queen on cardboard in windows up and down the street. Flags flying too.

No bunting, mind you.

Kate smiled at that memory before going on to say, "We had one family who thought they were a bit more upmarket than the rest of us. They did put up some bunting across the street before the coronation. Back then we never normally had much in the way of traffic. Then, out of the blue, a great big lorry came along and went straight through the bunting. We thought it was hilarious."

Nobody was laughing too much, however, when the heavy clouds began to gather over Derby on coronation day itself – just as the open-air party outside the flats at the top of Exeter Street was about to start.

The Melbourne sisters had changed into new dresses made by their mother. They already had coronation tea spoons that had been given out at school. "We also had little hats with the Queen's head on," Sheila suddenly remembered before Kate pointed out that all the children also had coronation mugs. "But they were handed out at the street party."

It didn't last long. Those gathering clouds were now sending down rain that soaked the sandwiches and diluted whatever was in those mugs. Never mind the games. It was time to head to the Exeter Arms. And not just the men.

*****

We'll soon be heading back to the pub to reflect on what it was like then, how it has changed over seven decades and how it hasn't. But first let's find out what happened to the Melbourne family.

They didn't stay in the street too long after coronation day. Just as well, perhaps. The houses would soon be demolished. Meanwhile, the Melbournes would soon be going up in the world – up to an apartment atop a branch of Barclay's where John Melbourne had secured a job some sixteen miles away in the middle of Nottingham. "He'd seen the opportunity to have a better standard of living," Kate explained. "But the flat we lived in, on St Peter's Gate, seemed enormous to us."

For all the comparatively modern facilities, however, it seems that neither sister was too pleased by their sudden elevation.

"I hated it," Sheila shuddered. "By then I'd got to the age when I had quite a few friends back in Derby. But here we were in a centre of a city where there was nobody of our age living nearby."

Kate felt much the same, it seemed. "I loved going back to Derby at weekends to stay with my auntie."

But time moves on and so did the family – to another branch of Barclay's in the Nottingham suburb of Mapperley where the bank was "like our front room". Life improved. They made new friends. They went to better schools. And eventually they went to work, Sheila as a short-hand typist at the city's health department and Kate as a nurse who finished up as a care home inspector.

Both still live on the edge of Nottingham to this day, Sheila in Arnold to the north of the city and Kate in the borough of West Bridgford, just south of the Trent. She shares a substantial house and expansive garden with her long-time husband, John Holmes MBE.

The award, presented by Prince William rather than the late Queen, was for charity fund-raising on a large scale. John had been a producer on BBC Radio 4 and he put a few jobs my way in my freelance days. But we'd met during my long-ago brief spell as a news producer on Radio Nottingham where he was already a star presenter with his own show.

He'd kept a surprisingly long silence as his wife and sister-in-law had rummaged through their memories of coronation day. That may be because, as he put it eventually, "I don't remember the day much at all". And that may be because events as shown at great length on the broadcasting corporation that would later employ him didn't quite live up to the build-up.

"I was six at the time and living in Leigh-on-Sea (in Essex). I'd been given a cut-out of Buckingham Palace and a toy coronation coach. The only other thing I recall about the day is my parents telling me, 'You should remember this. It may not happen again in your lifetime'."

*****

We met up again a few days after our reunion in West Bridgford. Sheila and Kate were back in Derby at the Exeter Arms, the only surviving building from their childhood apart from the flats across the road where the coronation street party had been rained off.

By the time our delayed train arrived, John was seeing off a "Thai-inspired egg noodle soup" from an extensive menu that also included Korean fried wings and a Kashmiri cod and prawn curry. Back in the "good old days" of the 1950s the best you could have hoped for would be a packet of Smith's crisps with a little bag of blue salt that tended to cling to one crisp above all, no matter how much you shook the bag.

Yes, things had changed in the Exeter Arms. The table that I'd reserved was in the extension built into what had once been the house next door and the home of the local "bookie". But there were still things that hadn't changed.

Kate and Sheila were soon standing in the bar and pointing to the step leading up to the preserved snug with its curved benches. "And that's where the piano was," Sheila pointed out before Kate pointed to the door through which they used to lean to listen to the parrot's choice words and their mother used to stand waiting for a jug of pub-brewed ale on Sunday lunchtimes. It's now the front door and, no, you can no longer lean through a top half.

But there's still a hearth with an open fire. And there are still hand pumps on the bar next to all kinds of keg beers and lagers from near and far. No, the draught beer is no longer brewed on the premises. But it hasn't come far. Most of those pumps project various ales from Dancing Duck Brewery. And that's based in Derby.

Step outside the pub and traffic is roaring past on flyovers and underpasses.

Cars were something of a rarity on Exeter Street of the early 1950s. Lorries were even rarer. Apart, that is, from the one that brought down the bunting stretched across the street before the coronation.

Ironically, that long-gone street has long been a car park. Hoardings ranged around it, however, suggest that one of the many redevelopment projects being planned by Derby City Council could be underway one of these days.

Sheila and Kate lived most of their subsequent lives in a different world in a different city some sixteen miles down the road. There is, though, one relic of the street where they started out in life. The blue plaque screwed to the outside wall of the house next door is now on another wall just above the doorway of the Exeter Arms.

It's dedicated to Herbert Spencer, no less, who was evidently born there in 1820. He became, according to the plaque, a "philosopher, radical pioneer, sociologist, educationalist and supporter of Charles Darwin". Yes, the Charles Darwin who came up with the theory known as "the survival of the fittest".

Spencer, incidentally, was fit enough to survive until he was eighty three, by which time he lived a long way from Derby.

This book has featured the celebrations around the coronation of a Queen who "did her bit" in the war and her duties over many decades since. But she was born into wealth and privilege that most of us could never imagine. So were her descendants, including her eldest son who may or may not have been crowned by the time some readers reach this point.

Herbert Spencer, on the other hand, is one of many examples of someone making something of his life, despite having been born in a humble nineteenth-century terraced street.

The same could be said of Aneurin Bevan, who was started life in a Welsh mining village yet went on to found the National Health Service that helped many of the unfit survive.

Perhaps we as a nation should raise a glass, if not a flag, every now and then to the "nobodies" who become "somebodies". Most, if not all of them, are even more worth celebrating than those who were, apparently, "born to reign over us".

Regulars ready for a day out from the Exeter Arms in the early fifties

A rare visit inside the Exeter Arms for women and children on coronation day

BIOGRAPHY

Chris Arnot has written fourteen non-fiction books. *Small Island by Little Train* was published by the AA in 2017 and shortlisted for the Edward Stanford awards for travel writing the following year. Marcus Beckmann called it "very much a state-of-the nation book" in his *Daily Mail* review.

Chris also wrote four of the *Britain's Lost* series for Aurum. *Britain's Lost Cricket Grounds* was reprinted twice after some glowing reviews. The late Frank Keating described it as "a coffee-table classic for and of posterity" in the *Guardian* and Jim Holden hailed it as "the best sports book of 2011" in the *Sunday Express*. Billy Elliot creator Lee Hall called *Britain's Lost Mines* "an extraordinary gallery of lives and landscapes".

As a national freelance journalist for a quarter of a century or so, Chris wrote for the *Guardian*, the Independent, the *Observer*, the *Times* and the *Telegraph*. And, until lockdown, he was a regular contributor to the *Sunday Telegraph*'s Pint to Pint column, a collection of which was published in 2016.

Other Books by Chris Arnot

The Archers Archives (co-written with Simon Frith)
(BBC Publishing, 2009)

Fields of Dreams
(Step Beach, 2012)

Britain's Lost Cricket Grounds
(Aurum Press, 2011)

Britain's Lost Breweries and Beers
(Aurum Press, 2012)

Britain's Lost Mines
(Aurum Press, 2013)

Britain's Lost Cricket Festivals
(Aurum Press, 2014)

The Day We Won the Cup
(Step Beach, 2015)

Small Island by Little Train
(AA Publishing, 2017)

Thanks Shanks
(Takahe Publishing, 2017)

The Festive Soul of English Cricket
(Takahe Publishing, 2019)

Larkin About in Coventry
(Takahe Publishing, 2018)

Decline and Fall to Rise and Shine
(Takahe Publishing, 2020)

Closing Time
(Takahe Publishing, 2021)